Bangor Street Railway

FEW HISTORIES are the work of but one person and the author is happy to extend grateful acknowledgement to the following who have rendered valuable assistance in the preparation of this work:

O. R. Cummings of Manchester, New Hampshire, who has produced so many fine histories of other Maine street railway systems, for his whole-hearted cooperation in providing much pertinent data and many photographs of the Bangor system.

Vincent Trincia of Sanford, Maine, for his permission to make use of portions of his original thesis on the subject of the corporate structure of the associated Bangor railway and power companies.

The late Guy Webster, long-time motorman on the Bangor trolley cars, for many rare clippings and photos of the original Bangor Street Railway, as well as personal recollections of the system's operations.

Certain veteran officials of the Bangor Hydro-Electric Company who were kind enough to review this manuscript and for their generous loan of photographs from the company's files.

And special acknowledgement and sincere thanks are extended to Bangor's number one trolley enthusiast, Miss Louise M. Prince, corresponding secretary of the Bangor Historical Society, for her close cooperation over many years in locating sources of material and in tracking down veteran employees to be interviewed. Truly, without the continued support and encouragement of Miss Prince this history could not have been written.

The usual available sources were, of course, utilized, such as the Maine Railroad Commissioners' Reports, Maine Public Utilities Commission Reports and such files of the Bangor Daily News and the Lewiston Journal as were available to the author.

To all those mentioned, and the many others who have contributed bits and pieces of information, have suggested other sources of research, offered criticism, or provided photographs or other data, one can but offer a most grateful "thank you."

CHARLES D. HESELTINE
445 Preble Street
South Portland, Maine 04106

Transportation Bulletin

A publication of Connecticut Valley Chapter, Inc., of the National Railway Historical Society, Inc. Editor, Roger Borrup, P. O. Box 232, Warehouse Point, CT 06088.

Printed by the Wadsworth Press, Warehouse Point, Conn. Ken Sheldon, pressman; Roger Borrup, compositor.

No. 81.　　　　　　　　**January-December 1974.**

ISBN (International Standard Book Number) 0-910506-17-5
Copyright 1976 by Roger Borrup and Charles D. Heseltine.

WHILE THIS ISSUE is being dated for 1974, printing is actually being finished in January 1976. No. 82 "Hyde Park Division, Bay State Street Railway" will be dated for 1975, although it will not be issued until well into 1976. Following that will be No. 83 "Stamford Street Railroad" dated for and issued in 1976.

BANGOR, MAINE—A summer scene at Market Square in 1890.

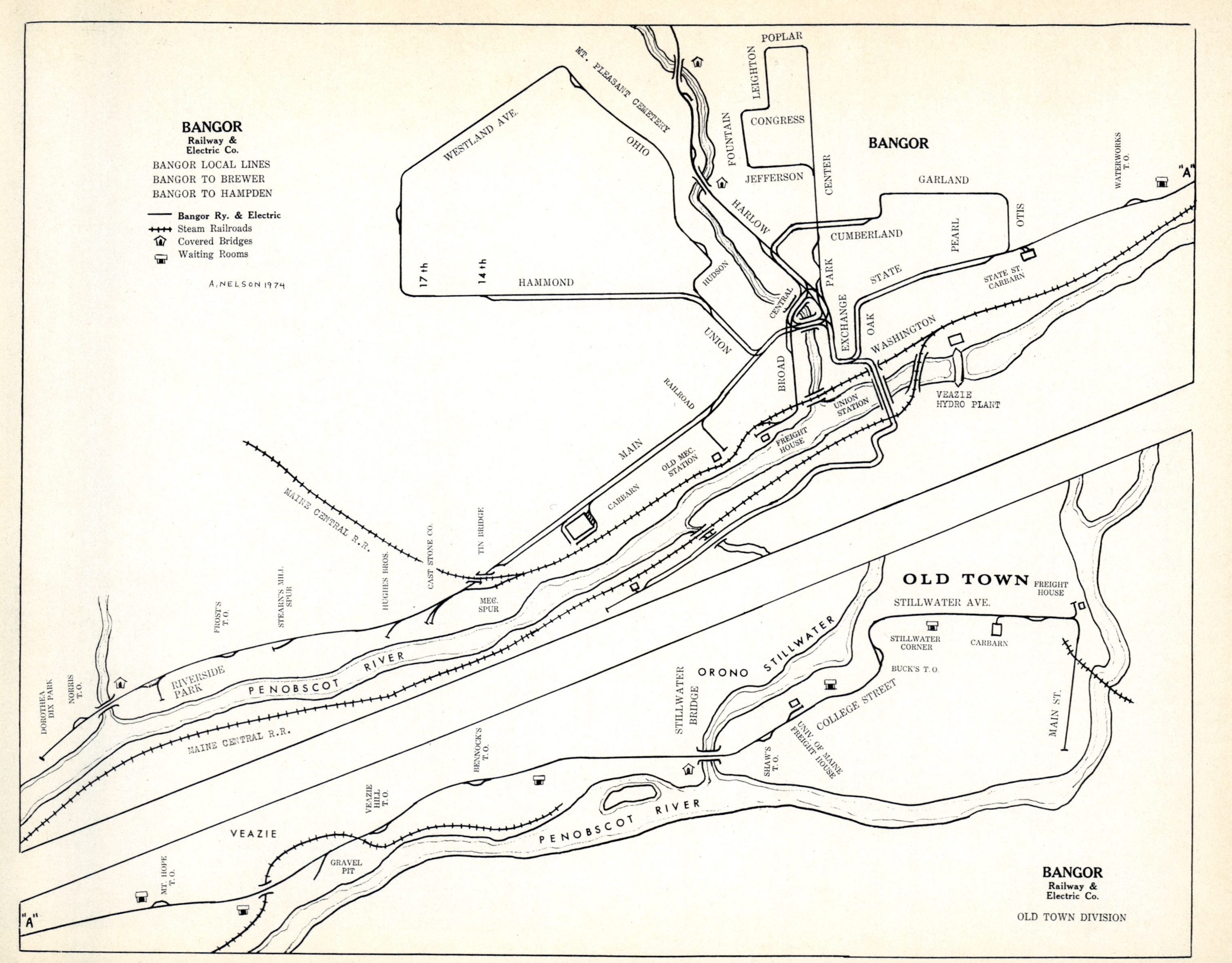
BANGOR
Railway & Electric Co.
BANGOR LOCAL LINES
BANGOR TO BREWER
BANGOR TO HAMPDEN

Bangor Ry. & Electric
Steam Railroads
Covered Bridges
Waiting Rooms

A. NELSON 1974

BANGOR

POPLAR
LEIGHTON
CONGRESS
JEFFERSON
FOUNTAIN
HARLOW
CENTER
PARK
GARLAND
CUMBERLAND
STATE
PEARL
OTIS
WATERWORKS T.O.
"A"
STATE ST. CARBARN
EXCHANGE
OAK
WASHINGTON
VEAZIE HYDRO PLANT
MT. PLEASANT CEMETERY
WESTLAND AVE.
OHIO
17th
14th
HAMMOND
HUDSON
UNION
CENTRAL
BROAD
RAILROAD
MAIN
UNION STATION
FREIGHT HOUSE
OLD MEC. STATION
CARBARN
MAINE CENTRAL R.R.
HUGHES BROS.
CAST STONE CO.
TIN BRIDGE
MEC. SPUR
FROST'S T.O.
STEARN'S MILL SPUR
RIVERSIDE PARK
PENOBSCOT RIVER
MAINE CENTRAL R.R.
DOROTHEA DIX PARK
NORRIS T.O.
BENNOCK'S T.O.
VEAZIE HILL T.O.
VEAZIE
GRAVEL PIT
MT. HOPE T.O.
"A"
PENOBSCOT RIVER
STILLWATER BRIDGE
ORONO STILLWATER
SHAW'S T.O.
UNIV. OF MAINE FREIGHT HOUSE
COLLEGE STREET
BUCK'S T.O.
STILLWATER CORNER
CARBARN
OLD TOWN
FREIGHT HOUSE
STILLWATER AVE.
MAIN ST.
BANGOR
Railway & Electric Co.
OLD TOWN DIVISION

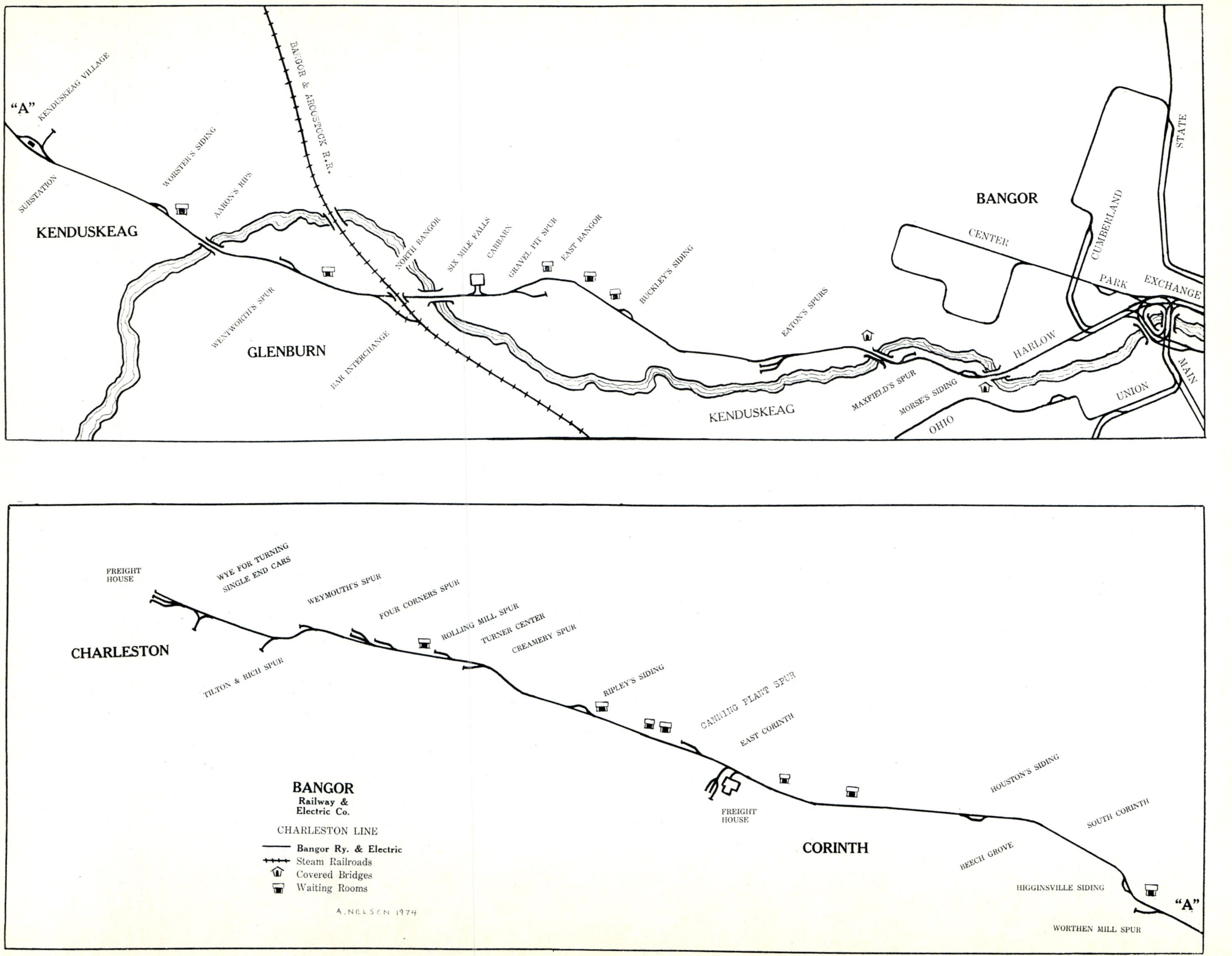
"A"
KENDUSKEAG VILLAGE
BANGOR & AROOSTOOK R.R.
SUBSTATION
WORSTER'S SIDING
AARON'S RUS
KENDUSKEAG
WENTWORTH'S SPUR
GLENBURN
TAR INTERCHANGE
NORTH BANGOR
SIX MILE FALLS
CARBARN
GRAVEL PIT SPUR
EAST BANGOR
BUCKLEY'S SIDING
EATON'S SPURS
KENDUSKEAG
MAXFIELD'S SPUR
MORSE'S SIDING
OHIO
BANGOR
CENTER
CUMBERLAND
STATE
PARK
EXCHANGE
HARLOW
UNION
MAIN

FREIGHT
HOUSE
WYE FOR TURNING
SINGLE END CARS
WEYMOUTH'S SPUR
FOUR CORNERS SPUR
ROLLING MILL SPUR
TURNER CENTER
CREAMERY SPUR
CHARLESTON
TILTON & RICH SPUR
RIPLEY'S SIDING
CANNING PLANT SPUR
EAST CORINTH
FREIGHT
HOUSE
HOUSTON'S SIDING
SOUTH CORINTH
CORINTH
BEECH GROVE
HIGGINSVILLE SIDING
"A"
WORTHEN MILL SPUR

BANGOR
Railway &
Electric Co.
CHARLESTON LINE
Bangor Ry. & Electric
Steam Railroads
Covered Bridges
Waiting Rooms
A. NELSON 1974

BANGOR RAILWAY & ELECTRIC COMPANY
MILEAGE TABLE
Computed from Market Square, Bangor

CHARLESTON LINE

Frt. House to Market Sq.	*0.43
Market Square to:	
Morses Siding	0.81
Maxfield's Spur	1.25
Eaton's Spur	1.61
E. Bangor Gravel Pit	2.53
Six Mile Falls Car Barn	3.56
N. Bangor BAR Spur	4.48
Wentworth's Spur	6.52
Worster's Siding	8.68
Kenduskeag Village Sid'g	11.17
Higginsville Siding	13.24
Houston's Siding	15.89
E. Corinth Freight House	19.31
Canning Company Spur	20.00
Ripley's Siding	21.11
Turner Centre Creamery Spur	22.62
Robbin's Mill Spur	23.01
Four Corners Spur	23.88
Weymouth Spur	24.55
Tilton & Rich Spur	24.71
Charleston Freight House	25.01
End of Track, Charleston	25.82

OLD TOWN LINE

End Double Track, State Street	1.21
Waterworks Siding	2.09
Mt. Hope Siding	3.52
Gravel Pit Spur	5.40
Veazie Hill Siding	5.92
Bennocks Siding	7.57
Stillwater Bridge	9.03
Shaw's Siding	9.61
Bucks Siding	11.41
Hospital Siding	13.08
Old Town	14.28
Great Works	15.54

STATE STREET LINE

Brewer Branch-off	0.40
End Double Track, State	1.21
Cumberland Street T. O.	1.99
Market Square	2.91

GARLAND STREET LINE

Cumberland Street T. O.	0.92
Double Track, State St.	1.70
Brewer Branch-off	2.51
Market Square	2.91

CENTER STREET LINE

Park Street T. O.	0.35
Jefferson St. Branch-off	0.99
Loop	2.01
Park Street T. O.	2.65
Market Square	3.00

BREWER LINE

End Double Track, Washington Street	0.54
Center Street T. O.	0.87
Grove Street T. O.	2.29
End of Line	3.27

HAMPDEN LINE

Union Street Branch-off	0.18
Car Barn, Main Street	1.26
End Double Track	1.48
MEC RR Interchange	1.73
Cast Stone Co. Spurs	1.88
Hughes Bros. Spur	2.24
Leary's T. O.	2.37
Frost's T. O.	3.95
End of Line (11/39)	6.14
Dorothea Dix Park	6.81

OHIO STREET LINE

Union Street Branch-off	0.18
Hammond St. Branch-off	0.46
Chatham Street T. O.	0.66
17th Street T. O.	1.76
Westland Avenue T. O.	3.07
Webster Avenue T. O.	4.22
Union Street	5.09
Main Street	5.09
Market Square	5.27

HAMMOND STREET LINE

Union Street Branch-off	0.18
Hammond St. Branch-off	0.46
Webster Avenue T. O.	1.05
Westland Avenue T. O.	2.20
17th Street T. O.	3.51
Chatham Street T. O.	4.61
Hammond Street	4.81
Main Street	5.09
Market Square	5.27

LIGHTWEIGHT CAR NO. 16 is shown in this picture on a layover in Brewer where the cars changed ends on a grade.

Chapter 1

Bangor Street Railway

Although the city of Bangor, Maine—"The Queen City"—was a bustling commercial center in the late 'Eighties with a population of nearly 20,000 citizens, it lacked any form of public transit such as had been developed in other areas of the Pine Tree State.

Horse car lines served Portland, Biddeford, Saco, Old Orchard Beach, Lewiston and Auburn, Waterville and Fairfield, and even the small town of Fryeburg. The steep hills of Bangor apparently had discouraged the use of animal power for a street car line, although a short-lived omnibus line had served outer State Street for a brief period. Bangor cast its lot with the new and wonderful electric cars then being perfected.

Throughout the 1880s around the country various attempts to provide electric street railway service were being made. As early as 1884 there were electric cars in the city of Cleveland, Ohio; in South Bend, Indiana, in 1885; Scranton, Pennsylvania, and Montgomery, Alabama in 1886; and a line in Asbury Park, New Jersey in 1887.

In fact, no less than 10 electric street railways were in operation along a total of some 60 miles of track by the end of 1887.

These early lines were pioneer ventures, and service was spasmodic. It remained for Richmond, Virginia, to open the first truly city-wide electric car system on February 2, 1888. This generally is credited as being the first truly successful operation of its kind.

Even before this opening, however, the citizens of Bangor were preparing for their own electric line which would place that city as the first in the state of Maine to enjoy electric car service.

A company known as the Goff Electric Co. had been organized in the early 'Eighties for the manufacture of electric current and was the forerunner of the power and transportation system which served Bangor over the years.

Goff was shortly joined by Frederick M. Laughton and George N. Ross and the company was reorganized as the Bangor Electric Light & Power Co. on May 2, 1885. The first power house, a steam generating station, opened in a 3-story building at Cross and Columbia Streets in the fall of 1885.

Equipment for this plant was purchased from the Thomson-Houston Co. of Lynn, Mass. The infant industry was capable of providing all manner of electrical apparatus, but was badly in need of customers.

To aid in providing for the establishment of power companies, Thomson-Houston furnished this equipment partially for cash and partly in return for blocks

BANGOR STREET RAILWAY NO. 10 is shown about 1901 at Birch Hill (Highlands was the later destination name). The numbers 10, 11, 12 and 13 were given to the city's first electric street cars. The crewmen are N. Pierce and William Henry.

of securities in the various projects. In this fashion, the Bangor Street Railway and the local power interests came under domination of the Thomson-Houston Co. which became part of the Edison-General Electric Co. As will be brought out, General Electric held a sizable interest in the Bangor properties for many years.

The beginnings of the street railway operations in the city of Bangor date to January 4, 1887, when five prominent citizens, Frederick M. Laughton, Eugene M. Hersey, Robert F. Straine, Frederick W. Hill and Charles E. Hill, presented a petition to the city government seeking permission to lay tracks in the public streets for an electric (or horse) railway.

The application was referred to a special committee which included the mayor, two aldermen and three city councilors for investigation. At a meeting held January 18, 1887, the city council approved the project and endorsed the proposed charter. The new company, to be known as the Bangor Street Railway, was duly incorporated by the state legislature on February 11, 1888, and the act, included in Chapter 97 of the Private and Special Laws of the State of Maine, was signed by the governor four days later.

Among the provisions of the charter was one stipulating that at least 1½ miles of track was to be completed and ready for operation within one year, unless the company was granted an extension by the city council.

The act of incorporation also specified that the franchise and locations should be granted for a term of 25 years—but that it might be renewed from time to time. Also it provided that other street railways might connect to the Bangor Street Railway's tracks and use its rails. Capital stock was limited to $300,000.

The franchise granted by the city of Bangor was dated June 10, 1888, and contained the following provisions:

Whenever there shall be snow or ice to the depth of 6 inches or less, said company may remove the same from their tracks by shovels or ploughs, or such means as the street commissioner shall approve; provided they level it off and grade outside the rails so as to allow sleighs and other vehicles to pass along and across said streets and over their rails with safety and convenience. But if such consent for removing ice or snow is not given, or if said company prefers not to incur the expense of such removal or grading, then such company shall be authorized, but not required, to use a sufficient number of sleighs or other carriages, or to mount their cars on runners, to do their business over their route until cars can be used on their tracks.

No car shall be drawn or propelled on their road at a speed greater than 6 miles an hour.

Whenever cars are turning a corner from one street to another, the speed will not be greater than if drawn by horses at a walk.

The conductor and driver of each car shall keep a vigilant watch for all teams, carriages, vehicles, patrons on foot, especially for children, and, upon the least appearance of danger to such teams, carriages, vehicles or persons, the cars shall be stopped in the shortest possible time.

The conductors shall not allow ladies or children to enter or leave the cars while in motion.

No salt or other articles shall be used in removing snow or ice from their tracks which may prove injurious to sleighs or other vehicles passing along or crossing them.

The route chosen for Bangor's first electric line commenced at a point near the "Tin Bridge" close to the East Hampden town line, and extended northeasterly along Main Street to West Market Square and the municipal bridge over the Kenduskeag Stream, through State Street to Exchange, down Exchange Street to Washington, along Washington Street to Oak, up Oak Street to State and along State Street to Pearl Street. This route was selected to avoid the steep grade of State Street Hill.

The "Tin Bridge" mentioned at various times in this narrative was a wooden span built by the Maine Central Railroad to carry its tracks over the highway. It was covered with sheet tin to protect it from the elements. However, dry rot set in beneath the metal sheathing and in 1871 it collapsed beneath the weight of an early Pullman train. Although replaced over the years by more substantial spans, it is still locally referred to as the "Tin Bridge."

Early in July, 1888, it was announced that construction of an electric line would shortly commence. The firm of Gore & Woodward of Boston was awarded the contract for the roadbed and the laying of rails, while Thomson-Houston was to erect the overhead wire and provide the generating equipment.

The Thomson-Houston Co. had agreed to accept an interest in the new company as partial payment for its services. An order for four 16-foot closed passenger cars, each accommodating 22 seated passengers, was placed with the Newburyport (Mass.) Car Company.

Actual construction commenced at 6:30 a. m. on Thursday, August 16, 1888, with Mr. Laughton, the president of the company, turning the first spadeful of earth at the lower end of Main Street. Tracklayers closely followed the grading party, using 35-pound tram rail along the entire route. Rails had reached the Bangor House within two weeks and a branch track was laid down Railroad Street to the old Maine Central depot to facilitate the hauling of the rails from the steam road.

NO. 12 BANGOR STREET RAILWAY with original type trolley pole. This car was first electric in Maine. Crewmen are O'Brien and Coombs.

By early October, track building had been completed, except for aligning some of the curves along the way. The overhead wire was all in place by late November.

The summer of 1888 had been a rainy one which hampered construction work and much difficulty was experienced with the mud of Bangor's streets. During the early years of operation, the poor foundation of this line, coupled with the very light rail, provided handicaps to the efficient operation of the system.

A wooden "car-stable" was built on outer Main Street near Dillingham Street, on land purchased from the Katahdin Ice Company. This carbarn had but one entrance door. A transfer table within the building permitted movement of cars from one track to another. (The Rockland, Thomaston & Camden Street Railway also used this same arrangement at its Rockport carbarn). Within a short time, however, increasing traffic required that the Bangor barn be rebuilt with a door for each stall.

The street railway company made arrangements with the Bangor Electric Light & Power Co. (of which Mr. Laughton also was president), to install generating equipment at the Cross Street station. The station at that time had a direct current generator with a capacity of 395 lamps. (It was then the practice to rate a power plant by the number of lamps it could provide power for). The equipment for the street railway operation consisted of an Arlington-Simms steam engine belted to a Thomson-Houston D-62 (75 Kw) generator with steam to be provided from the boilers already installed.

One car was on the property by early December, 1888, and it is apparent that some tests of it had been made within the carbarn, as a news item reassured citizens that "no serious damage to pocket watches has been experienced in the testing of the electric car." Electricity, it must be remembered, was still a somewhat mysterious force at that time!

The contractors, desirous that the official opening of the new street railway be made under the best of circumstances, and perhaps concerned with talk of the so-called "Bangor winters," felt it to be in the best interests of all parties to wait until spring before putting the road into operation.

For this reason, they released a generator on order for the Bangor road to the West End Street Railway of Boston, Mass., and it was not until March, 1889, that the new generating equipment arrived and was installed.

Even as the final touches were being applied to the line and the electrical equipment checked out, the Bangor Street Railway on March 12, 1889, received legislative approval to build a line in neighboring Brewer which had just been incorporated as a city.

A privately owned, wooden, covered toll bridge spanned the Penobscot River connecting Bangor with Brewer. The street railway company made several

NO. 12 REPAINTED and with more modern type trolley pole. Car was being used on isolated Brewer Division in this view.

offers to the bridge company for the right to lay rails across the ancient span, but without success.

It was proposed by the railway management to remove 100 tons of slate from the roof and to replace it with sheet tin so as to offset the weight of the electric cars. However, the street railway never was able to make use of this bridge and the Brewer line operated as a separate division until the opening of a substantial municipal bridge in 1914.

In the franchise providing for the operation of the Brewer Division, it was stipulated that rails might approach the toll bridge no closer than 50 feet at either side. The Brewer line also was given permission to close down if winter storms made operations difficult, a provision made use of on this section of line as no snow plow was available for clearing the rails.

The countless delays in getting the Bangor line into operation drew pithy comments from the editors of the day, one observing:

> President Laughton did not start the cars today (April 1st). Several reasons were given. One is that the snow storm prevented. Another that there is too much mud on the rails. But the principal reason is that today is All Fools Day, and so many people have been fooled so many times as to the opening date, that the time appeared improper!

As a result of the continuing delay in the opening of the road, the city council on April 3rd directed that the city solicitor notify the Bangor Street Railway that it had forfeited its charter. Some arrangement must have been made, however, as nothing more relative to this subject was heard.

By April 5, 1889, the large engine for the street railway's power plant had arrived and was hauled to the Cross Street station by oxen. Three more closed cars were on the property and had been equipped with motors and controls. Final alignment of the rails was being carried out by the contractors. The track had settled in some spots during the winter and a road scraper was required to scrape the mud from the rails for the entire length of the line.

Three weeks later the newspapers were reporting "signs of life" as regards the street railway. Citizens of Bangor were becoming impatient for an opportunity to ride the new electric cars.

The first trial trip over the Bangor Street Railway was made shortly after midnight on the morning of April 29, 1889, the following account coming from the Bangor Whig and Courier:

> At about twelve o'clock last night, the first trial trip was made over the electric railway and everything worked out to the apparent satisfaction of the managers. It was rumored Saturday that a trial trip would be made that night and many were about the streets anxious to see the first electric car move over the road. Yesterday the new engine at the power station was started up, as everything worked well, it was decided to make a trial trip at night when the streets would be free of teams.
>
> Mr. Laughton, Mr. E. J. Winslow, an expert from the Thomson-Houston Co., and those who were to have charge of the road after the cars are running, met at the carbarn on the Hampden Road and waited for the power to be turned on. The car used was No. 12, which weighs 11,250 pounds.
>
> When the current was on, the car was started and moved smoothly, reaching Cedar Street in about ten minutes. No trouble was experienced from any of the curves. When Washington Street was reached, and the car had gone

NO. 29 at Birch Hill on the Ohio Street line, ready to go downtown.   Crewmen are Ernest Barker and William Nickerson.

nearly around the curve from Exchange Street, the power failed and the car stopped. It was learned that the drive belt at the power station had slipped off its pulley.

The current was soon turned back on again, and the car moved over the whole distance to Pearl Street, three miles in about thirty minutes. The return trip was made without difficulty.

Few people were about at that time of the night and the novel sight was therefore enjoyed by only a limited number of people but now that the first trial trip has been made everybody will be on the lookout for the cars to commence running regularly in the daytime.

Additional trial trips were run on subsequent days, regular service being delayed by the weather and trouble at the power house. At first, the engine bearings overheated and then the piston became disabled, and there was some trouble with the generator. Finally, two cars were put into operation on May 21st, with a third being added three days later to provide a 20-minute headway. The fourth car was held at the car-barn for a spare.

These four original cars were of the closed type, with open platforms at each end in the same fashion as horse cars, with the crews being exposed to the weather in all seasons. (It was not until 1906 that the state legislature required the vestibuling of all electric cars).

The cars sides were of the conventional convex-concave panel type characteristic of the period. The cars had rectangular monitor roofs. There were five drop-sash windows on each side. The inside of the passenger compartment measured 16 feet in length. Bangor cars were originally painted yellow.

Motor equipment consisted of two F-30 motors manufactured by Thomson-Houston, with double reduction gears. Controls were of the Model 51 rheostat type. The trolley pole was of wood, made of two grooved pieces of hardwood, wired together with No. 4 wire in the center. The trolley wheel had to be oiled at the end of each run, while the line crew greased the overhead trolley wire every week with petroleum jelly.

"Captain" Joseph Wentworth was the road's first motorman, the first conductor's name was Pierce.

A timely warning appeared in the local papers shortly after the road went into operation. It was food for thought!

It behooves the people who transport gunpowder through our streets to keep at a safe distance from the electric cars. The stream of fire which follows the cars for some of the time would prove a serious obstacle in the way of a cartload of powder! This is only a suggestion, there would, however, be money in the pocket of those who heed it!

From the foregoing, it would appear that the new road was none too well bonded to provide for proper current return through the rails. A heavy copper wire cable had been laid along the center of the track with each individual rail connected to it to provide for the current return. Later methods of rail bonding proved much superior.

The cars "went on vacation" June 4th, when the armature of the dynamo gave out and had to be turned down. This work was performed by the Union Iron Works of Bangor which handled all of the company's

BANGOR STREET RAILWAY original No. 20, built 1890, ready for a run via State and Main Streets to the Highlands.

heavy repair work until the new and modern carbarn and shops were opened in 1906.

There were other interruptions and frustrating shutdowns of the road, mainly due to trouble at the power house, but each time service was restored as quickly as possible. Following one such delay, one newspaper commented:

People who were left way down on the Hampden Road do not believe strongly in the electric road tonight!

Headlights of the kerosene type, similar in appearance to those used on steam locomotives, were first used June 22nd and were highly acclaimed. Until then, cars had been operating at night without headlights. There were no lights within the early electrics, either.

On the night before July Fourth, 1889, the cars ran until very late, with all four cars out on the line. So late did they run, in fact, that operations did not commence until mid-morning "in order that the company might rest its men."

On the holiday, two open cars which had arrived but had not been fitted with electrical equipment, were pressed into service as trailers. Some 4,346 riders were counted on the Fourth of July.

The Bangor Street Railway was 3 miles in length, with three turnouts to permit the passing of cars. There were many sharp curves and grades, the most severe curve being of 35-foot radius on a 7% grade. One ¾-mile stretch had five curves and an average grade of 5%. Nonetheless, the cars had little difficulty in negotiating the route.

Thirty minutes were allowed for the running time, a formal timetable going into effect July 11th, providing for a car every 20 minutes from 6 a. m. until 11 p. m. The fare was 5 cents.

Although two of the new open cars were on hand in time to be used as trailers on the Fourth of July, they did not commence to operate under their own power until July 26.

The four closed cars were numbered 10, 11, 12 and 13, while the first four open cars were numbered 14, 15, 16 and 17. Late in the fall a fifth closed car arrived and it was numbered 18. This was slightly longer and had one additional window on each side. It was equipped with a coal stove to provide heat in cold weather.

It was the practice of the Bangor Street Railway to number their cars consecutively as they arrived on the property, with replacements taking the number of the car being replaced.

VEAZIE HYDRO STATION on the Penobscot River was first developed in 1889 to supply power for Bangor's trolley cars. It was one of Maine's first hydroelectric plants. Car No. 52 shown in photo was placed on the site as a workman's shelter.

In a general renumbering which took place under Public Works Co. management shortly before the turn of the century, open cars were given odd numbers and closed cars even numbers. Even so, Bangor seemed ever reluctant to use new numbers and, in some cases, there were as many as four different cars over the years which had carried the same number.

With the same numbers listed on various rosters throughout the years, it accounts for the discrepancies which must appear on even a studiously compiled list of rolling stock.

State Fair Week in September, 1889, provided another busy time for the new electric road, with 8,200 passengers hauled during one day of the fair. It was reported by the press that one conductor registered 160 fares during a single trip. All this despite an obstacle to through operations caused by the rebuilding of the State Street bridge over the Kenduskeag Stream.

At the time that Bangor's first trolley line began operations, workmen began placing the foundation for one of Maine's first hydroelectric plants. This was for the Bangor Light & Power Co. and was located a short distance up the Penobscot River in Veazie. It also was intended as a source of power for the street railway as the Cross Street station was proving inadequate.

The new hydro station called for additional financial arrangements and the Public Works Co. was chartered October 19, 1889, to provide for the management and closer relationship among the various water power, electric light and street railway lines in operation or planned in the Bangor area. Securities of the Public Works Co. were passed, in return for the new electrical equipment, to the supplier, the Thomson-Houston Co.

In October, 1889, Elias Chesrown, former electrician for the company, was named to succeed W. S. Bolton as superintendent of the Bangor Street Railway.

A waiting room was opened on Main Street in West Market Square for the convenience of the public. In front of the station, cars for the Main Street line clanged their gongs once before starting, and the cars for the State Street line clanged their gongs twice.

When storms or other delays tended to put the cars off schedule, a printed sign was displayed in the waiting room window indicating the cars were operating on a 30-minute headway instead of the regular schedule. With the arrival of the fifth closed car, the normal headway was increased to 15 minutes.

During the four months and 10 days of the Bangor Street Railway's operations from May 21 to September 30, 1889, the road reported to the Maine Railroad Commission that it had carried 215,547 passengers, with receipts of $11,434.00 and net income of $5,356.00.

Snow-fighting equipment did not arrive in Bangor until November 14, 1889, but it indicated that the company planned to operate during the winter months

VEAZIE HYDROELECTRIC STATION INTERIOR as it appeared in the early 1920s is shown in this official photograph.

if possible, despite provisions in its charter for the optional use of sleigh cars.

This snow-fighting equipment was furnished by Dorner & Dutton Co. of Cleveland, Ohio, and included horse-drawn snow levellers, snow scrapers or "flangers" which were fitted beneath each closed car, and a 4-wheel snow plow.

This plow had no electrical equipment and was intended to be pushed ahead of a motor car. This proved to be too severe a task on the motor car and for the balance of the winter the plow was hauled over the line by a team of 10 horses.

The following winter the plow was fitted with motors and carried the number 40—again being numbered consecutively following receipt of additional passenger equipment during 1890. There was but one interruption in service that initial winter noted in the press, which stated that the cars "were stalled all over the city."

With the coming of spring and the successful operation of the original line an accepted thing, steps were taken to expand the system. Construction of the line between Brewer and South Brewer commenced June 2, 1890. On June 18th the Ohio Street line was begun from a connection with the Main Street line, through Union, Hudson and Ohio Streets to Birch Hill near Mount Pleasant Cemetery.

The company had proposed using High Street, but certain influential citizens who had homes there successfully opposed this choice. With these lines under construction, the company also built a short extension from the junction of Washington and Oak Streets to the Bangor end of the toll bridge.

The Brewer Division extended from a point near the exit from the toll bridge in Penobscot Square, through Center Street and along North and South Main Streets to a point near Stone Street, close to the Brewer-Orrington municipal line. A wooden carbarn, 60 x 20 feet was constructed at this end of the route. Rails ran along the side of the highway the entire way.

In late August, 1890, two cars were carried over the Maine Central Railroad bridge to Brewer and placed on the street railway tracks. On the morning of September 1st, following three trial runs, regular service commenced on an hourly headway, with one car in operation. Power for the Brewer Division was furnished by the newly-opened Veazie station.

A test run over the Birch Hill line was made September 11, 1890, and regular service started the 14th. This line of cars ran from Mount Pleasant Cemetery to the Bangor end of the toll bridge. There were three turnouts on the line, one at the foot of George Street, one at Hammond and Union Streets and one opposite the Children's Home.

Power for this line initially came from the Cross Street station, but as soon as the new line from Veazie could be cut in, power was supplied from that facility.

Some minor troubles were encountered at the new Veazie plant at the beginning and power was cut back and forth between it and the old Cross Street station until finally the old generating plant was shut down permanently October 8th.

With the opening of these new routes, the Bangor

"NEWBURYPORT" CAR NO. 32 at carhouse in South Brewer—one of the 21 cars purchased in 1890 and one of the first two assigned to the isolated Brewer-South Brewer line when it was opened in 1890. Note the old type of wooden trolley pole.

Street Railway had 7.25 miles of track as follows: Main Street-State Street line, 3.13 miles; Birch Hill (Highlands) line, 1.53 miles; Brewer line, 3.50 miles.

During the fiscal year ending September 30, 1890, the company reported a total of 616,258 passengers for a total of $30,189 in receipts and a net profit of $8,632. Car tickets, not unlike those in use on the steam railroads, were issued on the several lines.

The track within the city of Bangor was mainly in the center of the various streets. In Brewer it followed the side of the highway. A 400-foot trestle had been constructed on the Brewer Division over a small creek, elsewhere the trolley made use of municipal bridges.

During 1890, to provide rolling stock for the new routes, the company took delivery of 10 additional closed cars and 11 open cars, making a total of 30 passenger cars on the property.

Although they had been ordered from the Newburyport Car Co., it is known that a portion of this order was "farmed out" to the Ellis Car Co. of Amesbury, Mass., but which cars is not known. The cars, however, were

always referred to as "Newburyport" cars. Numbered consecutively as they were received, the closed cars were Nos. 19, 20, 21, 30, 34, 35, 36, 37, 38 and 39. The open cars were Nos. 22, 23, 24, 25, 26, 27, 28, 29, 31, 32 and 33.

In a move to improve the financial structure of the company, and in keeping with the management of the street railway by the Public Works Co., deeds covering

ORIGINAL CARBARN on Main Street was a wood stable-type building with a one-track entrance and a transfer table inside—within two years modified into multiple-door structure shown in small view.

the Bangor Street Railway were passed to Charles A. Coffin, representing the Thomson-Houston Co. July 15, 1891.

To improve the status of the various Bangor interests, a further reorganization took place in 1894 to knit the separate companies still closer together. This was required as a result of the reorganization of the Edison-General Electric Co. with the backing of the J. P. Morgan Co. of New York City.

As General Electric held large interests in various lighting and power companies as well as street railway enterprises, a move was made to weld them into more solid corporate structures. Coffin, who was president of General Electric, held control of the stock of the Public Works Co. until 1901, disposing of his holdings at that time to other stockholders of General Electric.

No further extensions of the street railway were built until 1893 when track was laid from the junction of State and Exchange Streets, through Harlow, Cumberland and Center Streets, a distance of about one mile, to the corner of Center and Congress Streets. The line was approved for operation June 3, 1893.

The same year—1893—five of the closed cars were scrapped by the company. Early electric cars were little more than motorized horse cars and they quickly reached the point of obsolescence. One new closed car was purchased in 1894. Two former open horse cars were secured second hand from the West End Street Railway of Boston in 1895 to be run as trailers. They had been numbered 1759 and 2169 on that system, but the Bangor numbers are not known.

During 1895 tracks were laid from a junction of the Ohio Street line on Union Street, the length of Hammond Street as far as Fourteenth Street, a distance of about a mile. The Bangor, Orono & Old Town Railway, then being under construction and having in mind its eventual route into downtown Bangor via Otis, Garland and Cumberland Streets, caused the Bangor Street Railway to revise its line serving Center Street through the laying of rail from State and Exchange Streets up Park and Center Streets to Cumberland Street, in place of its former routing.

The Main Street line was double tracked as far as Maplewood Park as a result of the projected Bangor, Hampden & Winterport Railway which secured trackage rights to West Market Square. The State Street line was extended several hundred feet from Pearl to Otis Street to connect with the Bangor, Orono & Old Town road and rail was extended on Main Street from the "Tin Bridge" to the East Hampden town line.

BREWER-SOUTH BREWER CAR NO. 13 is shown in late fall, 1890, waiting at toll bridge terminus—bridge in background. The crewmen in the photo are Mann and O'Brien. The Brewer line operated without track connections to Bangor until 1914.

As of June 30, 1896, the Bangor Street Railway reported 8.4 miles of main line, 1.3 miles of second track and .10 mile of sidings and turnouts, for a total of 9.8 miles of line. Four 16-foot closed cars were secured second hand from the West End Street Railway in 1896, the original numbers being 1380, 1388, 1438 and 1489. These were for use as trailers.

No. 1438 had been built by the Jones Car Co. of Watervliet, N. Y., and the other three by J. G. Brill of Philadelphia. Although initially used as trailers, they were later equipped with motors.

The company disposed of one more closed car in 1897 and rebuilt one of its open cars into a work car. One more closed car was retired during 1898. In 1899, a new open car was purchased, presumably to replace the one rebuilt for work service. One ex-horse car of the closed type was sold to the Penobscot Central Railway for use as a passenger trailer behind its gasoline-electric motor.

There were no changes of rolling stock during 1900, the company operating 13 closed and 15 open cars. During 1901, two closed cars and two open cars were retired. A general renumbering of the cars of the various lines managed by the Public Works Co. took place about this time, but, unfortunately, old records which would aid in reconciling the old and new numbering systems were lost when the company's general offices were destroyed in the Great Bangor Fire of 1911.

In August, 1902, President Theodore Roosevelt was a visitor to Bangor. So popular was this Great American in the Queen City, that the street railway was hard pressed to handle the crowds which turned out to see him and all but one car was out on the line. A frantic call was sent out to the one remaining car crew which happened to be on vacation and as soon as the two men could be rounded up, every bit of rolling stock of the company was at work from mid-morning until midnight.

During 1902, the Bangor Street Railway, under Public Works Co. management, extended the Center Street line from the junction of Center and Congress Streets through Center to the corner of Poplar Street. This line was further extended through Poplar, Leighton, Congress, Fountain and Jefferson Streets back to a connection at Center Street to form a loop operation. The new trackage opened on August 13, 1904.

This marked the final construction work of the Bangor Street Railway, which, unlike the majority of city street railways, built no suburban lines of its own, other than the Brewer Division. It remained for the consolidation of 1905 to place the suburban lines, together with the city routes, into one integrated system.

In an effort to assist patrons on the Brewer Division in making connections between street cars at either end of the toll bridge, and to eliminate operation of electric cars up to the Bangor end of the span, the company purchased two electric automobiles of the sight-seeing type late in 1901 and placed them in service from the corner of Washington and Oak Streets,

DOWNTOWN BANGOR IN WINTER, December of ▮▮▮▮ with cars Nos. 12 and 18 in original paint schemes with name of contractor on the dashers, passing on Main Street turnout in Market Square. Cars have their original wooden trolley poles.

which became known as "Brewer Junction," across the bridge to Penobscot Square in Brewer.

This, without doubt, constituted the first "bus" service in the Pine Tree State—if not in New England. It was, however, a short-lived affair, for the freshet of March, 1902, carried away one of the wooden center spans of the toll bridge.

As a result, the cities of Bangor and Brewer, acting under a provision of the charter given the bridge owners, took over the remaining portions of the bridge and replaced the washed-out section with a substantial iron structure. The remaining wooden sections still were ruled out for use by electric cars. During the period when the bridge was closed to traffic, a small steam ferryboat plied back and forth between the two cities and trolley service was adjusted to this arrangement.

To provide rolling stock for the newly-opened Center Street loop and as replacements for older cars, the company took delivery of seven single truck 18-foot closed cars in 1903 from the Brill Co. These cars were numbered 14, 16, 18, 20, 22, 24 and 26 as it was the continued policy of the company to retain original car numbers when making replacements. These cars were all equipped with vestibules and were hand-braked.

Four open cars were transferred to the Bangor Street Railway during 1904 from the Bangor, Orono & Old Town Railway. Although built as single truck, 10-bench cars, they had been equipped with double trucks of the maximum traction type. The large semi-convertibles of the Old Town road acquired in 1902-03 were more adaptable to the 15-mile suburban run.

The Old Town open cars had been renumbered 51 through 65 (odd numbers) by the Public Works management and those turned over to the Bangor local system were assigned to the Hampden run which served popular Riverside Park.

June 30, 1905, was the date of the consolidation at which time the various water power, electric light and street railway properties were reorganized in a merger creating the Bangor Railway & Electric Co.

At that time, the Bangor Street Railway reported 9.069 miles of main track, 2.671 miles of second track and .60 mile of sidings for a total of 12.84 miles. It held trackage rights totaling 1.49 miles over lines of connecting companies, operating 14 closed and 17 open cars.

Chapter 2

Bangor, Orono & Old Town Railway

About two years after the Bangor Street Railway was chartered, the Old Town Street Railway was incorporated by the state legislature and was authorized to build a line from the center of Old Town to Upper Stillwater Village and to Great Works Village.

Incorporators of the company, which was chartered March 9, 1889, included Joseph L. Smith, James Weymouth, Flavius O. Beal, Albert O. Brown, James W. Sewell, William F. Pearson and William Engel. Capital stock was $100,000 and the road was empow-

OPEN CAR NO. 3, one of eight original opens of the Bangor, Orono & Old Town Railway when it began operating in 1895.

ered to suspend operations during the winter months or at any other time when the wants of the public did not require its operation.

The company was permitted to operate omnibuses in place of street cars. (For a short time prior to the opening of this road, a horse drawn omnibus line served outer State Street, but whether it was affiliated with the proposed electric road or not cannot be determined).

An amendment to the Old Town Street Railway's charter provided that it might also build from Old Town through Milford and Bradley. This was approved by the legislature February 27, 1891, but the line was never built through these places. Corporate life of the company was extended in 1893 until February 9, 1895.

The Old Town, Orono & Veazie Railway chartered by the legislature February 26, 1891, with permission to build from a connection with the Old Town Street Railway, through Orono to Main and Olive Streets in the town of Veazie. Here it was to connect with a proposed extension of the Bangor Street Railway.

The Old Town, Orono & Veazie's charter provided that, if the Bangor Street Railway failed to build into Veazie, the new company might extend its line from Main and Olive Streets in that town, toward Bangor.

On the other hand, if the Old Town, Orono & Veazie road did not build within a two-year period, the Bangor Street Railway was granted rights to extend through Veazie and Orono to Old Town. It appears that in seeking charters no one was overlooking any bets!

Incorporators of the Old Town, Orono & Veazie Railway included A. J. Durgin, B. E. Coniga, E. N. Mayor, A. F. Lewis and Albert White, all of Orono; A. J. McPhetres, A. Lambert, E. K. Stuart and J. E. Kent of Veazie and J. Manchester Haynes of Augusta.

Capitalization was set at $500,000 and, like the Old Town road, it could suspend during the winter months if it saw fit.

The Old Town, Orono & Veazie was permitted to lease all of its property and franchises to another company if it so desired, or it might acquire by lease or purchase the property and franchises of any other street railway whose line was constructed or chartered so as to form a connecting or continuing line with its own.

Acting upon this proviso, the Old Town, Orono & Veazie took the Old Town Street Railway under lease on June 15, 1892. Neither line, at this time, had started construction.

Under the Special and Private Laws of the State of Maine for 1893, Chapter 559, the Old Town, Orono & Veazie road received permission to change its name to the Bangor, Orono & Old Town Street Railway, with authorization "to build from Veazie into Bangor along State Street, thence through Howard, Pearl, or some other convenient street between the last two named, thence through Garland Street to Center, through or

NO. 53 of the Bangor Railway & Electric Co. as shown in this view at Hampden Lower Corners originally was a **10-bench single truck open car** of the Bangor, Orono & Old Town Railway. Open cars of this type were assigned to the Hampden line.

across Center Street to and through Willow, Market, Curve, Harlow and Central Streets, or by such other equivalent and convenient route. . . from said State Street, to West Market Square in Bangor."

Nothing was done toward the construction of this railway until the entrance of Amos F. Gerald into the picture in late 1894. Amos F. Gerald was one of the foremost street railway promoters in Maine, being the backer of the Portsmouth, Kittery & York Street Railway, the Lewiston, Brunswick & Bath Street Railway, the Skowhegan & Norridgewock Railway, the Bath Street Railway, the Waterville system and several others.

A resident of Fairfield, Gerald in association with Isaac C. Libby secured control of the Bangor, Orono & Old Town charter and arranged for the financing. Like the Bangor Street Railway, it is apparent that the Thomson-Houston-General Electric combine was instrumental in supplying much of the needed equipment under the usual terms of a block of securities as a major payment for services rendered.

The route of the Bangor, Orono & Old Town Street Railway commenced at the junction of State and Otis Streets in Bangor, where a carbarn was erected, along State Street to the Veazie town line, continuing along the County Road in Veazie where it crossed at grade the Maine Central's main line to Vanceboro, thence along the highway to the Orono town line, crossing the Maine Central again at grade just before reaching this point.

Entering Orono at Veazie Hill, the line followed County Road and Main Street to and over the double-barrelled wooden covered bridge spanning the Stillwater River, thence along Bridge and College Streets, passing the campus of the State College (University of Maine), to Stillwater Village, thence along Stillwater Avenue to Main Street in Old Town, and southerly along Main Street to Great Works Village at a point near Main and Jameson Streets.

Fifty-two pound rail was used in building the line, which followed the side of the road throughout. Construction proceeded rapidly and on July 9, 1895, the railroad commissioners granted a certificate of safety for the trackage from State and Otis Streets in Bangor to Main Street, near Center, in Old Town.

Cars commenced running on July 17th through to Old Town, although some service had been provided as far as Veazie two weeks earlier. The road had acquired trackage rights from State and Otis Streets into downtown Bangor over the rails of the Bangor Street Railway which had extended its track from Pearl to Otis Streets to effect this connection. The new line was 13.25 miles in length.

At the time of opening, the road had six single truck closed cars numbered 9 through 14. They were equipped with vestibules as protection against the weather. The eight single truck 10-bench open cars were numbered 1 through 8. (These cars were later fitted with maximum traction double trucks). There was a single truck snow plow, with a second plow being added a short time later.

The main carbarn was at State and Otis Streets in Bangor and a small, one-stall barn on Stillwater Avenue near the hospital in Old Town provided storage for the late-night car. Power was provided from the Veazie hydro station. A storage battery bank was provided at Old Town to help maintain power in that area, fed from a small generating station across the river in Milford.

Concerned with the hazardous grade crossing in Veazie, the Railroad Commission on November 6, 1895, ordered the street railway to construct an overhead crossing and recommended that the highway also be changed at the same time. The town was ordered to pay for the cost of the highway relocation, with the street railway paying two-fifths and the Maine Central Railroad three-fifths of the cost of the combined highway-trolley span.

This structure was completed during 1898, but the town did not complete its end of the bargain—relocation of the highway—until 1901 and until that time the street railway could not use the facility.

Reports of the city electrician of the city of Old Town for 1895 and 1896 reveal complaints that the street railway had attached its span wires for holding up the trolley wire to buildings on Main Street and to trees along Stillwater Avenue, a practice felt to be improper. He further complained that four different utility companies were using four separate sets of poles for their lines through Old Town and recommended that a plan be worked out to provide one substantial set of poles for all wires.

On June 3, 1896, the street railway was granted permission to cross the Bangor & Aroostook Railroad's tracks at grade on Main Street in Old Town and a certificate of safety for the extension of the road to Great Works Village was issued July 18, 1896. Operations over this new line did not commence at once, and the service over this end of the route was intermittent for several years.

"BAND CAR" was the name applied to this express car purchased from the West End Street Railway of Boston in 1895 by the Public Works Co. for Bangor, Orono & Old Town Railway's projected freight business.

PHOTOS ON PAGE 19 AT THE RIGHT SHOW—

Snow-fighting equipment which was depended upon to keep line to Old Town open in early days.

No. 76, one of the six double truck Brill semi-convertibles bought for the Old Town line in 1902, faced the camera with its crew at end of the line.

B. O. & O.

76

The Bangor, Orono & Old Town experienced some difficulty in making its scheduled time with the single truck closed cars. When they arrived in Old Town far behind schedule the cars often did not continue on to the end of the line in Great Works Village; thus there were many complaints. It was not until after arrival of the double truck semi-convertible cars that the Railroad Commission could report that "this portion of the road was being operated with regularity and dispatch."

Taking advantage of its charter rights to gain access of its own into downtown Bangor, the Bangor, Orono & Old Town Railway built a line through Otis, Garland, Essex and Cumberland Streets in 1897. This connected with previously laid track of the Bangor Street Railway at Center and Cumberland Streets with the latter company ceding rights to this rail as well as that along Harlow Street. The latter company had already relocated its Center Street line through Park Street in anticipation of this project. Sixty-pound "T" rail was used along with 90-pound girder rail where required. The new route was approved July 5, 1897.

In conjunction with this project, rail also was laid along Central Street and across the municipal bridge spanning the Kenduskeag Stream, from Harlow Street into Market Square at Main Street. There was opposition to the operation of electric cars on Central Street and, for this reason, the company elected to wait until late on a Saturday night to accomplish its purpose.

A small army of laborers was recruited quietly and they appeared at the appointed hour with scrapers and teams. It was a time when the municipal authorities were powerless to locate a judge who would order the work stopped by issuing a restraining order.

Working by torch light, the crew plowed up the gravel street surface, dropped in their ties and spiked down the rails. The entire stretch was resurfaced by daylight! While city fathers and police looked on helplessly, a diamond crossing was built over the tracks of the Bangor Street Railway and rail was laid along Broad Street for several hundred feet to be used as a terminus for the Old Town cars.

With their new track in place, the company could report a total of 16.7 miles of line in operation, one-half mile of which was in sidings and turnouts. It also had trackage rights over the Bangor system amounting to 1.2 miles. Cost of the completed road was $229,885.

A further addition to its operational mileage came when the Penobscot Central Railroad built from the end of this line on Broad Street, through Broad and Front Streets to the Boston & Bangor Steamship wharf. This track was leased to the Old Town road for a venture into the trolley freight and express business.

Officials in 1897 were: Amos F. Gerald, president and general manager; I. C. Libby, treasurer; A. J. Durgin, clerk; Ivan L. Meloon, superintendent. Gerald apparently gave up his interest some time during 1898, becoming involved in the development of the Lewiston, Brunswick & Bath Street Railway. Meloon became associated with the Atlantic Shore Line Railway. The

BUCKING SNOW on the way to Old Town before the advent of the big rotary snow plow in 1901 and the double truck cars.

Bangor, Orono & Old Town Railway passed into the hands of the Public Works Company in 1898.

The old wooden Stillwater Bridge which had been strengthened for the weight of the electric cars at the time of the road's construction worried the Railroad Commission. As early as 1897, it reported that additional repairs had been made, and in reports for the next few years concern was expressed as to its safety.

The bridge was strengthened in 1900 with additional arches and trusses, but ultimately was declared unsafe for the cars and it was substantially rebuilt.

A double truck rotary snow plow was acquired in 1901 and the smaller of the two conventional plows was disposed of, presumably to the Penobscot Central. That road was converted to trolley overhead in 1901 after failure of their experiments with a gasoline-

COVERED BRIDGE over the Stillwater River at Orono through which the trolley cars on the Old Town line ran until 1912.

ROTARY PLOW purchased in 1901 by the Public Works Co. management to cope with heavy snows on the Old Town line.

electric motor car. The Bangor, Orono & Old Town purchased two additional single truck closed cars about the same time.

The single truck closed cars proved to be an unhappy choice for the long 16-mile suburban run and the riding public was not long in expressing dissatisfaction as to the riding qualities of the vehicles! They were dubbed "teeter-tails" from the name of a shore bird said to stand in the sand and rock back and forth. There also were some less polite appellations applied to these cars!

Their continued use culminated in a midnight visit to the one-car storage barn at Old Town by nocturnal callers—students from the State College, legend has it —loaded with combustibles of all kinds, along with a few odd sticks of dynamite. The resultant conflagration obliterated both car and carhouse! The carbarn was not rebuilt, although the company retained the land until 1920.

Apparently the company "got the message." In 1902 six 28-ft. double truck semi-convertible cars began arriving from the J. G. Brill plant in Philadelphia. These were easy-riding cars and proved adaptable for the long run, becoming the first in a series of somewhat similar cars that were used on the Old Town Division.

Used year-round, the new and faster cars replaced both the open and closed single truck equipment. Four of the open cars were transferred to the Bangor Street Railway by Public Works management and two others were disposed of—to the Penobscot Central Railroad, it is thought. Only two open cars were retained on the roster.

In the general renumbering scheme of the Public Works Company, the single truck Old Town cars had been given the numbers 52, 54, 56, 58, 60, 62, 64 and 66, while the semi-convertible cars were numbered 68, 70, 72, 74, 76 and 78. The open cars were renumbered 51, 53, 55, 57, 59, 61, 63 and 65. The single truck closed cars disappeared from the scene at an early date and their final disposition has not been confirmed.

One source relates that the bodies were hauled to various sites along the Penobscot River for use by company officials as summer camps and, indeed, several may be found there today (1973). At some point, the single truck open cars were equipped with maximum traction trucks and saw service on the run to Riverside Park.

Thirty-minute schedules were maintained on the Old Town run, with the line being divided into three 5-cent fare zones. The frequent service offered by the electric railway cut heavily into the Maine Central Railroad's traffic between Bangor and Old Town and the steam railroad fought back through the operation of a "scoot" train running hourly between the two places, stopping on signal at nearly every crossroad and advertising competitive fares. After a few years, however, the Maine Central gave up and only its regular trains provided service to Old Town.

At the time of consolidation on June 30, 1905, the Bangor, Orono & Old Town Railway was operating a total of 17.6 miles of main line, 1.4 miles of second track and 0.5 mile of sidings and turnouts, for a total of 19.5 miles. Rolling stock consisted of 6 double truck semi-convertibles, 2 single truck closed cars, 2 open cars, 1 work car and 2 snow plows.

No. 82, a Brill 30-ft. 8-in. semi-convertible car, is shown passing Mt. Hope Cemetery on the Old Town line in the late 1930s.

Chapter 3

Bangor, Hampden & Winterport Ry.

The Bangor, Hampden & Winterport Railway had its inception on March 29, 1893, when the Hampden & Winterport Electric Railway & Light Co. was chartered by the legislature and authorized to build electric railways and lighting plants in the towns of Hampden, Winterport, Frankfort and Prospect.

This electric railway was to connect with the Bangor Street Railway at the Bangor-Hampden town line near the "Tin Bridge" of the Maine Central Railroad. Incorporators of the company, which had an authorized capitalization of $500,000, included J. Manchester Haynes and George E. Macomber of Augusta, Fred Atwood of Winterport and Herbert L. Shepherd of Rockport, Maine.

Two years later, the incorporators secured a renewal of the charter from the legislature—dated February 21, 1895—and the authorization to operate both passenger and freight cars over the tracks of the Bangor Street Railway into downtown Bangor. The Bangor Street Railway was granted equal rights over the proposed Hampden line.

Construction began during the fall of 1896. By this time J. Manchester Haynes and his associates had disposed of their interests in the company to a syndicate headed by James Cutler of the Public Works Co., which controlled the Bangor Street Railway and which shortly thereafter took over the Old Town road. Thus upon completion of the new line, its operations were closely allied with those of the Bangor Street Railway.

A certificate of safety was issued by the Railroad Commission on December 11, 1896, for the first mile and one-tenth, extending from a connection with the Bangor Street Railway at the "Tin Bridge" to Stearns Mill in the town of Hampden. Operation began at once, the company leasing rolling stock from the Bangor Street Railway which also supplied the crews. Charles Johnson had the honor of being the first motorman on the road with Charles Smith as his running mate. Both were on hand for the final run in 1940.

Cars of the Hampden road used the Bangor Street Railway's tracks into downtown Bangor, terminating their runs at West Market Square. The company never had its own carbarn, even after acquiring its own rolling stock, using that of the Bangor system. An addition was built onto the Bangor barn for this purpose.

The name of the Hampden & Winterport Electric Railway & Light Co. was changed to the Bangor, Hampden & Winterport Street Railway on February 2, 1897. On March 27th of the same year, the company was authorized to build electric lines through Newburgh and Dixmont in Penobscot County and in Monroe in Waldo County, and also to run over rails of the Bangor Street Railway and on to the towns of Herman, Levant, Stetson and Exeter.

None of these proposed extensions was ever built, nor did the rails ever reach Winterport.

Another 3.4 miles of track—from Stearns Mill to

HAMPDEN, MAINE, with Bangor Railway & Electric Co. car No. 44 and crew posed for a post card photograph about 1910.

Hampden Lower Corner—was opened on November 8, 1897. No further construction was carried out by this company, although in later years the line was extended to Hampden Highlands and the Upper Corner.

A covered bridge over the Sourdabscook Stream was of Howe truss design. Track was 60-lb. "T" rail at the side of the highway on good ties and a well-ballasted roadbed.

The location of the private bridge over the Sourdabscook Stream was parallel to the highway span at the foot of two steep grades. Much difficulty was experienced with drifting snow at this point and the company rebuilt the span into a covered bridge.

One authority on New England covered bridges believes this to have been the only covered bridge built exclusively for street car use. Teamsters using the nearby highway were accustomed to let their horses run down one hill to gain momentum for the pull up the other, but the bridge-covering obstructed their view and they were loud in their complaints to the street railway. The side covering was removed after a short period of use.

As of June 30, 1898, the road owned 4.52 miles of main track, .88 mile of sidings and turnouts and held trackage rights of 1.61 miles into downtown Bangor. Included in the sidings was a spur line of .23 mile into Riverside Park, a company-owned pleasure resort.

Power was supplied from the Veazie hydro-station. Fare was a basic 5 cents, with the road divided into two fare zones. Frost's turnout was the end of the first zone.

The street railway opened Riverside Park June 15, 1898, and it became one of the most popular attractions in the Bangor area. An open air theater was built into the banks of the river which formed a natural amphitheater, admirably suited for the purpose. Weekly changes of program drew large crowds.

Boats were rented along the riverfront and there was a gay midway with attractions to appeal to young and old. Management prided itself on making every effort to keep the resort at a high standard.

Riverside Park proved to be a traffic stimulator and surprisingly it was the only trolley resort in the Bangor area. During its hey-day, many cars were kept busy hurrying pleasure-seekers to and from the resort. Like most trolley parks, it was located slightly beyond

COVERED BRIDGE over the Sourdabscook Stream was used only by trolleys on the **Bangor, Hampden & Winterport** line.

RIVERSIDE PARK:

Opened June 15, 1898, the park was a summertime mecca for Bangor area residents, with thousands of people riding the trolleys to get there.   The park closed down after 1916.

the initial 5-cent fare limit, which doubled the company's receipts.

One account tells of the attendant at the power house having to hold the circuit breakers in by hand for an hour at the end of the day, when so much current was being drawn by the many cars on this line.

The cost of building the entire road, including Riverside Park had been a modest $114,604.

The company began using its own equipment following completion of the line through to Hampden Lower Corner, although in the summer months it fell back on rolling stock borrowed from the Bangor Street Railway to aid in servicing Riverside Park.

Cars of the company were purchased from J. G. Brill and consisted of two single truck vestibuled semi-convertibles numbered 1 and 2, four single truck open cars numbered 3, 4, 5 and 6 and a single truck combination passenger and express car numbered 7. There also was one snow plow.

Two more single truck 10-bench open cars were purchased from Brill in 1899. They were numbered 8 and 9. In 1900 a set of double trucks of the maximum traction type were placed beneath the combination car. Later this car was transferred to the Charleston Division of the Bangor Railway & Electric Co. for use as a freight motor with yet another set of trucks. It was then numbered (first) 108.

Snow seems to have been the bane of the Hampden line as traffic during the winter months was light and cars were operated only on an hourly basis. It was thus difficult for the single truck snow plow to keep the road open. During 1899, the road was tied up for several weeks and crews had to use picks and shovels to make way for the plow, even resorting to ice chisels to break out the rails.

A near serious accident occurred on the line on the evening of January 7, 1905, when heavy rains caused a section of the track to be washed away near Stearns Mill. An inbound car operated by Motorman Braithwaite with Conductor Kelly left the rails and rolled down the embankment. As the only people aboard, they were shaken up but otherwise unhurt.

It was at the time of the evening outbound rush hour and had the accident occurred to the outbound car, which was due to arrive shortly afterward, such a mishap might have proven disastrous. The line was tied up for four days while temporary cribbing was erected to shore up the roadbed.

The Bangor, Hampden & Winterport Railway, at the time of the consolidation of June 30, 1905, had 4.52 miles of main line, 0.88 mile of sidings and turnouts, for a total of 5.40 miles. It had two single truck semi-convertible cars, one double truck combination car, six open cars of the 10-bench single truck type, two work cars and one snow plow.

SNOWDRIFTS were a common sight on the Hampden line in the winter. Here's one that had to be dug out by hand in 1899. Car No. 1 of the Bangor, Hampden & Winterport Railway is shown approaching a snow bank as high as trolley car itself.

Chapter 4

Penobscot Central Railway

The Penobscot Central Railway was one of the earlier projected suburban street railways extending from the Bangor area. On April 15, 1891, the citizens of the town of East Corinth held a special town meeting to vote upon an article calling for the issuance of bonds to a total of $16,400 with which to purchase stock in the proposed road. Other towns along the way followed suit.

Nothing was done in connection with building the road, so the 1894 town meeting at East Corinth considered a warrant "to see if the town is willing to appoint a committee, jointly with the town of Charleston and the town of Kenduskeag, to employ counsel and, if advisable, to institute action to recover money raised and paid by said towns to aid in the construction of the Penobscot Central Railroad." It was so voted.

At the 1895 town meeting in the same community, it was voted to leave in the hands of the selectmen the disposition of money furnished the Penobscot Central —if recovered. A proposition at the meeting the following year to see if that town would extend its credit to aid in the organization of the Bangor Suburban Railroad was rejected.

So, it would appear that this chapter of Bangor's street railway system did not get off to a very auspicious start.

Articles of association for the Penobscot Central Railway were approved on December 31, 1896, with Flavius O. Beal of Bangor, Isaac C. Libby of Waterville, Amos F. Gerald of Fairfield, Harrison F. Gould of Kenduskeag and C. E. Edmonds of Corinth as incorporators. Capitalization was for $250,000.

This company proposed to build from the Bangor-Glenburn boundary through Glenburn, Kenduskeag and East Corinth to Charleston, with a branch from Kenduskeag Village through Exeter to Garland, a total of about 35 miles. (The Garland branch never was built).

The original charter contained no provision for the road to enter the city of Bangor, but this was rectified by the legislature in 1897 which authorized the road to build from the Glenburn-Bangor line through the city of Bangor to the wharf of the Boston & Bangor Steamship Co. on Front Street.

Approximately four-tenths of a mile of track—from a connection with the Bangor, Orono & Old Town Railway spur on Broad Street to the steamboat wharf on Front Street—was completed by August 3, 1897. It was immediately leased to the Old Town road which was planning to develop a trolley freight and express service. The track crossed the main line of the Maine Central Railroad where an interchange track between the steam and electric roads was built.

Construction of the road northerly from Bangor started in the spring of 1898. The line began at a connection with the Bangor, Orono & Old Town Railway's line at Harlow and Cumberland Streets, leaving the city via Harlow, Valley and Kenduskeag Avenues.

Two wooden covered bridges were used to cross and recross the Kenduskeag Stream on the outskirts of Bangor, both spans being substantially reinforced for the weight of the electric cars and the prospective freight business.

From the outskirts of Bangor, the road generally paralleled the present-day (1974) Route 15 through North Bangor, Glenburn and Kenduskeag Village to

FIRST OFFICIAL TRIP TO CHARLESTON in 1902 was a gala occasion with the Penobscot Central's two large open cars and the former horse car trailer which had been fitted with double trucks. Here are the cars about to leave Market Square.

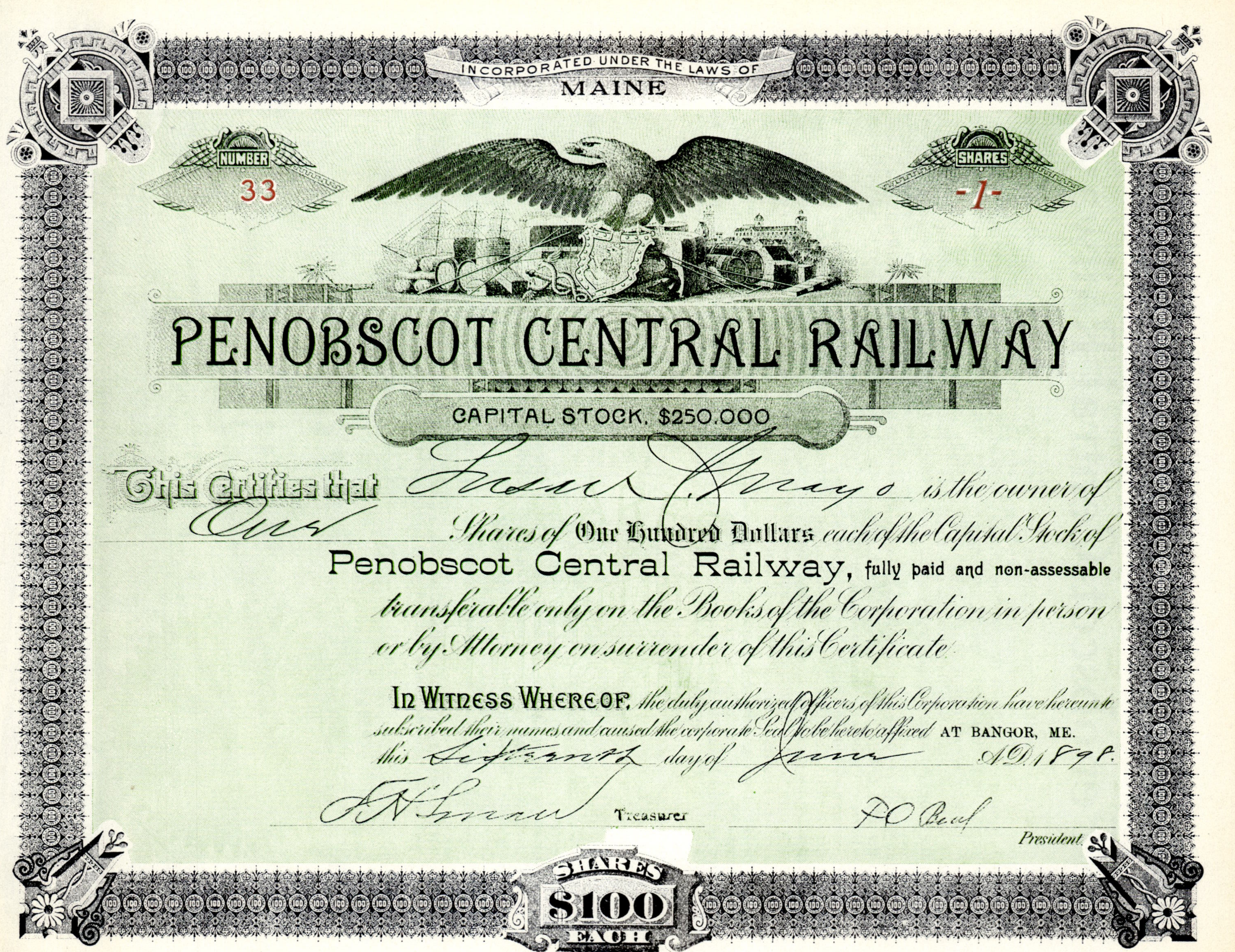

INCORPORATED UNDER THE LAWS OF
MAINE
NUMBER
33
SHARES
-1-
PENOBSCOT CENTRAL RAILWAY
CAPITAL STOCK, $250.000
This Certifies that Susan J. Gray is the owner of
One Shares of One Hundred Dollars each of the Capital Stock of
Penobscot Central Railway, fully paid and non-assessable
transferable only on the Books of the Corporation in person
or by Attorney on surrender of this Certificate.
In Witness Whereof, the duly authorized officers of this Corporation have hereunto
subscribed their names and caused the corporate Seal to be hereto affixed AT BANGOR, ME.
this Sixteenth day of June A.D. 1898.
Treasurer
President
SHARES
$100
EACH

the village of East Corinth, terminating about one-half mile beyond this point at a corn-canning plant.

A special town meeting in East Corinth on August 13, 1898, sought to determine on which side of the main street the railway would be permitted to build. As residents of neither side wished to have the tracks in front of their homes, a compromise was effected and the track was laid down the center of the street.

This solved the immediate problem, but as one old-timer recalled, it left the town with a poorly-graded Main Street until the rails were dug up some 35 years later.

Fifty-six pound "T" rail was used throughout. The line crossed the Kenduskeag Stream not only twice in Bangor, but also at Six Mile Falls at North Bangor and again at Aaron's Rips in Kenduskeag. At both of these points the railway built new spans; the one at Aaron's Rips was a combination highway-railway bridge for which the town contributed its share of the cost.

As the road was intended as a freight carrier as well as a passenger line, and it intended to haul standard railroad equipment, long radius curves and grades not over 5% were planned. However, the Railroad Commission ruled that the charter for the road determined that it was a street railway within the restrictive meaning of the term and that it must follow the highway throughout, except for one or two points.

The result was that grades as high as 10% had to be established and these proved difficult for the first motive power of the road to negotiate.

Instead of adopting the conventional overhead trolley system, the Penobscot Central purchased a Patton Motor Car, a self-propelled vehicle supplied by the Patton Motor Co. of Chicago. This car was an innovation in the railway industry which was finding some success on the open, flat lands of the Midwest.

Measuring 32 feet in length, the car was divided into two compartments, one for the power plant and one for the passengers. It was equipped with a 50 horsepower gasoline engine driving a 30 Kw direct current generator which supplied a bank of 110 storage batteries that in turn fed two 50 horsepower traction motors.

The generator and motors were the products of the Walker Co. of Cleveland, Ohio, and the car body was built by the Laconia (New Hampshire) Car Co. Christensen air brakes were installed, making it the first street car in Maine to be air-braked. The car weighed 56,000 pounds.

Enough of the road had been completed by late 1898 so that the Patton motor could be tested. On its first trip, the motor hauled a closed horse car purchased from the Bangor Street Railway which in turn had acquired it from the West End Street Railway of Boston. The

little train was reportedly greeted enthusiastically along the route by cheers, cannon and fireworks.

While the Maine Railroad Commissioners stated: "The use of this motor does away with power houses, overhead construction and the bonding of rails, and those in charge profess to be well satisfied with its performance," there was a bit of scepticism in this conservative praise.

Indeed, the motor did not turn out to be all that had been expected of it. The 10% grades were a considerable impediment. Gasoline engines had not been developed to peak efficiency at that early date and riding within the car itself was described as unpleasant due to the noise and vibration and fumes from the exhaust.

However, the gasoline engine, the generator and the 110 storage batteries left little passenger space at best and most people elected to ride in the trailer, even though being yanked along in an ex-horse car may not have been the acme of transportation comfort.

A certificate of safety for the 21 miles of track from Cumberland and Harlow Streets in Bangor to the railway's carhouse in East Corinth was issued December 17, 1898, but no regular service was started until June 8, 1899.

A report filed with the Railroad Commission covering operation of the road from that date through June 30 indicated a total passenger revenue of $102.55 and express earnings of $356.73—truly a modest start.

The company reported owning one Patton motor car, one former horse car, one snow plow, 10 box and

PENOBSCOT CENTRAL RAILWAY No. 1— Original Patton gasoline-electric motor car with horse car trailer on Kenduskeag Avenue, Bangor, is shown on a trial trip in 1898.

10 flat car trailers. The freight cars had been built by the Portland Locomotive Works.

No annual report was filed with the Railroad Commission for the year ending June 30, 1900. On April 7 that year the road decided to suspend operations and to adopt the conventional overhead trolley system. The sum of $105,000 was expended to rebuild the road. A steam power plant was constructed in Kenduskeag Village about midway on the line and a second carbarn was built at Six Mile Falls in North Bangor.

Some of the Bangor Daily News stories telling about the re-equipping of the Penobscot Central road during the fall of 1900 and early in 1901 make interesting reading:

September 24, 1900. Another large cargo of machinery arrived for the Penobscot Central power house at Kenduskeag Village. The cars, drawn by horses, started for Kenduskeag Village at the same time. There were 20 cars in all but the various teams got separated as they progressed over the line.

A fine new building has been completed at Kenduskeag Village and the machinery will soon be installed. Linemen have been engaged several weeks stringing wires from Kenduskeag Village to Bangor. Cars which used the Patton system are being rebuilt for trolley equipment at Six Mile Falls carbarn where the cars are stored.

(Actually there was only one car using the Patton system to be rebuilt.) Hauled by teams of horses, the freight car delivery of power house machinery must have made an unusual procession along the line. Spotting of three of the flat cars on the tracks in Harlow Street for several days led to an accident that resulted in a sheriff's attachment on the boilers that were being carried on the flat cars.

It seems that on the evening of September 26 a party of Bangor men was returning in a tally-ho from a day's outing at the Exeter Fair. In the dark, their driver ran into the freight cars and overturned his vehicle. Several men were injured; one of them, W. W. Palmer, receiving a broken leg. He had Sheriff Brown place an attachment on the boilers.

Progress on the power house was brought to a standstill until the railroad company could get a court injunction against the sheriff. The news articles go on to relate this and other news about the railway:

October 13, 1900. Progress on the Penobscot Central has been delayed. An attachment has been placed on the boilers due to the tally-ho accident on Harlow Street several weeks ago. The road might be in operation now, at least enough progress to run the ballast trains. As it is, President Beal does not know if the road will be in operation before November 15, the originally planned starting date.

The road has been leveled and lined up to within three miles of East Corinth. Ballasting is about done between Bangor and Kenduskeag Village. Poles are up to within two miles of East Corinth. Trolley feed lines and telephone wires are up from Morse's Bridge to Kenduskeag Village.

Painters have been working on the re-equipped cars and three of the four power cars have been made ready for use along with two passenger cars. Two plows have been built at the Union Iron Works of the steel plow-share point pattern. A private telephone line runs from company offices in Market Square to Six Mile Falls carbarn, Kenduskeag Village power house and East Corinth. Each car will have an attachment so that the conductor may use the telephone line at any point.

October 19, 1900. A temporary injunction has been granted against Charles H. Brown, the sheriff, removing the attachment on the boilers of the Penobscot Central which had been ordered by one W. W. Palmer. Penobscot Central now can continue its work.

November 16, 1900. But little remains to be done on the Penobscot Central. Wire is nearly all strung. Power temporarily is being supplied from the Veazie station for the work cars. Engineers completing the road and living at the Kenduskeag Hotel look like Weary Willies but with manners of Fifth Avenue. Bonding of the track continues.

EAST CORINTH waiting room was a busy place as open car No. 15 of the Penobscot Central Railway arrived from Bangor.

Work cars are being hauled by trolley. Work at the power house has been lagging but progress is being made.

November 24, 1900. Boilers are now being bricked in and the smoke stack has been raised.

April 8, 1901. Mr. Beal reports that the Penobscot Central could be put into operation tomorrow if there were need of it but operations should commence on regular schedules on the first of May. The power house has been tested and the rolling stock is ready to run. Tracks are in good condition but now require a last-minute going over due to the frost of the winter. A little snow remains, but should soon disappear. The road will end at East Corinth for the present, but the roadbed has been graded to Charleston. W. E. Pierce, formerly city electrician of the city of Bangor, has been named superintendent.

The schedule to be put into operation during the first weeks will be as follows: Leave Bangor at 7 and 10 a. m. and 2 and 5 p. m. Leave East Corinth for Bangor at the same time.

April 13, 1901. Power will be turned on at Kenduskeag Village for the first time Monday (April 15). Engines 1 and 2 have been run and broken in and worked satisfactorily. Engineer Landry and Assistant Engineer Cunningham have been hard at work and the work cars will now go out on the line to complete the track repairs. A regular schedule will commence May 3rd.

F. O. Beal is president, F. A. Hunt general freight agent and superintendent, William E. Pierce is superintendent of the electrical department, William Landry is chief engineer of the power house and E. E. Cunningham his assistant. Herbert Strout and F. Witham are the firemen.

Flavius O. Beal, president of the Penobscot Central, was also mayor of Bangor. In more than one newspaper article of the day, the railway was referred to as "Beal's Hoodoo."

The first electric cars over the line from Bangor reached East Corinth May 1, 1901. Twelve passengers were aboard the first car to leave East Corinth which departed at 6:30 a. m. with Conductor W. C. Noyes and Motorman Henry E. Stoker in charge. The northbound car was in charge of Henry Glasier as conductor and Ralph Weeks, motorman.

The arrival of the first electric cars into East Corinth about mid-morning caused students at the academy there to shout, "The electrics are coming! The electrics are coming!" And, according to one who was there, the building was vacated faster than any fire drill could have emptied it!

Regular schedules called for four daily round trips on weekdays and six on Sundays when special excursion rates were in effect. Running time was one hour and 20 minutes to East Corinth. Waiting stations were built along the route in true railroad fashion, being located at: Morse's Siding, Trigg's, Six Mile Falls, Miller's, Wyer's, Kenduskeag Village, Hudson Creek, Houston's, East Corinth and Collin's Mills. A siding was located at each of these points.

Cars left Bangor daily at 7:53 and 9:23 a. m., 2:30 and 5:15 p. m. There were two additional trips on Sundays as Beech Grove in the town of Corinth quickly became a favored picnic site for the residents of Bangor and way points.

Little information on the rolling stock of this line has become available, although it is known that they took delivery of two exceptionally large double truck steam coach roof open cars and two large double truck closed cars having smoking compartments. The old Patton motor was rebuilt as an electric freight motor and plow. Several cars apparently were acquired from the Bangor, Orono & Old Town Railway.

Regular fare to Kenduskeag from Bangor was 40 cents and to East Corinth 50 cents. These rates

SWITCHING FREIGHT at East Corinth on the Charleston line in the early days of the Bangor Railway & Electric Co. is first No. 108, which was originally a combination car on the Bangor, Hampden & Winterport Railway. Photo circa 1906.

were adjusted downward with the completion of the line into Charleston.

All cars of the Penobscot Central operated as "trains," down trains carrying odd numbers and up trains carrying even numbers. Down cars had the right of way and waited five minutes after normal leaving time at meeting points.

Up trains had that extra five minutes to make the scheduled meets; otherwise they had to keep clear of Bangor-bound trains. There were no protecting block signals on the road. Freight trains operated as "extras," keeping clear of all passenger runs.

The carbarn and freight house at East Corinth Village originally was built by a man named Hunting for a stage relay on the old Bangor-to-Greenville stage line. Later it was used as a depot for horses coming out of the woods before spending the summer in pasture. The firm of Morrison & Hunting, one of the large timber operators on the West Branch of the Penobscot River were the owners. The carbarn at Six Mile Falls was rebuilt from a former potato storage warehouse.

Within the city of Bangor the Penobscot Central had 5.72 miles of line. Overhead construction consisted of 13.12 miles of span wire and 13.13 miles of side bracket suspension. Except through East Corinth Village, the track was on the side of the highway.

The steam power plant at Kenduskeag Village was equipped with three boilers, two steam engines of 700 total horse power and two direct current generators of 375 Kw each. There also was a storage battery bank for auxiliary power.

A year went by before a certificate of safety for the 5.25 miles of trolley line between East Corinth and Charleston was issued on August 5, 1902. As of that date the Penobscot Central Railway owned 26.25 miles of main track, 1.06 miles of sidings and .25 mile of trackage rights within Bangor, for a total of 27.56 miles.

Fare to Charleston was established at 50 cents, the road being divided into ten 5-cent fare zones. The running time between Bangor and Charleston was two hours and the new schedule provided for five daily round trips for the passenger cars.

Total cost of the Penobscot Central Railway as of June 30, 1903, was $458,123 and its capitalization consisted of $250,000 in common stock and $250,000 in 20-year first mortgage 5% sinking fund coupon bonds dated December 2, 1901.

The State Street Trust Co. of Boston acted as trustees. There were 125 stockholders, 114 of whom with 1,150 shares were residents of the state of Maine.

The Penobscot Central served a very sparsely-settled region. The 1900 census gave a total of but 2,890 inhabitants within the towns of Glenburn, Kenduskeag, Corinth and Charleston. By 1910 the population showed a decrease of 3%, indicating that the area was less than a fertile field for a street railway.

Passenger service on the line was in keeping with the demand. Round trips diminished in number each year, with the following count: 1903—1,988; 1904—1,553; 1905—1,473.

Freight was the mainstay of the line as there was no steam road operating into most of the territory. Receipts from this source often exceeded passenger revenues. This business stemmed from the hauling of many carloads of lumber, canned goods, farm produce, wood pulp, fertilizer, hay, grain and potatoes.

A physical connection was available with the Maine Central Railroad in Bangor at Broad and Front Streets and standard railroad cars were handled over the line. Special links between couplers were needed on the rolling stock until it had cleared the downtown

NO. 1 OPEN CAR of the Bangor Railway & Electric Company circa 1910 on the Charleston line—a long ride on a 4-wheeler.

streets in Bangor and their curves. Shipments also were received from the Boston steamers at the freight house which was adjacent to the steamship wharf.

Total revenues failed to cover the cost of operation and fixed charges, and it was inevitable that the road should find itself in financial trouble. A substantial deficit had been incurred during three of the five years of operation.

As of June 30, 1903, there was a gross deficit of $147,562 of which $105,000 was the cost of converting to overhead current supply. Actual operating deficit was $40,695—much too heavy a burden to carry.

As a result of this poor financial showing, the road was unable to pay the bond interest due December 1, 1903, and was taken over by the bondholders. They instituted foreclosure proceedings and, in mid-1904, the property was sold at auction by the trustees, the State Street Trust Co. of Boston.

The purchaser was the Penobscot Central RAILROAD, an organization of the bondholders. They assumed formal control November 1, 1904.

In order that the larger steam railroad box cars might pass through the bridge at Aaron's Rips in the town of Kenduskeag, the railway had raised the lateral braces above the top chords of the span, apparently weakening the structure. Thus, when an over-sized box car struck one of the chords on August 18, 1904, the bridge collapsed and a temporary span was built in its place.

The newly-formed Penobscot Central Railroad protested that it was neither financially able—nor liable —to replace the damaged bridge. Following a lengthy hearing before the Railroad Commission, that body ruled that inasmuch as the new company intended to enjoy all the rights and privileges of the old, it also must assume its responsibilities and, therefore, must rebuild the bridge to the satisfaction of the town.

It was not, however, until 1907 that this was done and then by the Bangor Railway & Electric Co., joining with the town of Kenduskeag to provide a proper and substantial replacement.

The Penobscot Central Railroad did not last long as an operating company. Merely changing the name of the corporation did not make for any increase in traffic, although fixed charges were reduced. Maintenance had been poor and by 1904 the Railroad Commission was concerned with the condition of the track and roadbed.

Early in 1905 control of the road passed into the hands of the Public Works Co. in the form of a newly-organized corporation known as the Bangor & Northern Railway, which had been chartered by the legislature on March 15, 1905.

For all practical purposes, it became a part of the Bangor system, with power being supplied from the Veazie hydro station. The original steam plant at Kenduskeag Village was converted into a substation. The two companies were formally merged on January 31, 1906, when the road became the Charleston Division of the Bangor Railway & Electric Co.

No roster information has been found for the Penobscot Central. The two large double truck open cars apparently were disposed of shortly after the merger; the two large double truck closed cars went to the Waterville system where they became Nos. 24 and 25, after one of them saw service for a short time on the Brewer Division. Two freight motors, the rebuilt Patton motor and the former combination car of the Bangor, Hampden & Winterport saw some further service on the line, as did some of the single truck cars, both open and closed.

CAR FOR CHARLESTON—No. 32 was about to leave Market Square, Bangor, in 1915 as Conductor Arthur L. Cameron at left and Motorman William Wood at right posed for this picture. Brill combines Nos. 32 and 34 were regular cars on the run.

Bangor Railway & Electric Company

The Bangor Railway & Electric Company came into being in 1905. At that time there were a number of electric light, water power and street railway companies operating under the management of the Public Works Company, but representing a hodge-podge financial arrangement.

Individually, these various companies did not seem to have been making out too well financially. Of the 16 annual reports filed by the Bangor Street Railway, 11 of them indicated deficits. The Bangor, Orono & Old Town Railway had deficits in three of its nine operational years, while the Penobscot Central—or Bangor & Northern—was consistently in the red. Only the Bangor, Hampden & Winterport road managed to elude these deficits, and only by small margins in some years.

The General Electric Company, which held large interests in the Bangor corporations, organized the Electric Bond & Share Company in 1905 to take over GE's interests in the various enterprises throughout the country in which GE held large blocks of securities.

A move was then made to place these electric power and street railways on a more substantial footing. To this end, the services of John R. Graham were called upon to consolidate the Bangor properties. He was provided with the necessary backing through J. & W. Seligman & Company of New York City and E. W. Clark & Company of Philadelphia.

The predecessor of the Bangor Railway & Electric Company was the Old Town Electric Company which had been organized July 23, 1889. The name of the corporation was changed, by act of the legislature, on February 16, 1905. The act permitted the newly-organized Bangor Railway & Electric Company to purchase, or otherwise acquire, the various lighting, street railway and water power companies of the area.

This, of course, included the Bangor Street Railway, the Bangor, Orono & Old Town Railway, the Bangor, Hampden & Winterport and the Bangor & Northern. The latter, however, which had just undergone its second reorganization, was not officially brought into the fold until the following year.

The story of the Bangor Railway & Electric Company is the story of John R. Graham, a successful shoe manufacturer of Brockton, Mass., who had developed an interest in the street railway field. He had assumed control of the foundering Quincy & Boston Street Railway and within a short time had restored it to a prosperous utility which later became a part of the Bay State (later Eastern Massachusetts) Street Railway.

DOWNTOWN BANGOR looking west toward City Hall (with clock tower). The open trolley is about to head up Main Street.

He had served as vice-president of the Bay State, as general manager of the Brockton Street Railway and was a member of the first Rapid Transit Commission in the Commonwealth of Massachusetts.

Called upon to enter the Bangor picture on behalf of the General Electric Company, John Graham apparently found a challenge in the Queen City, and within a short time was serving as treasurer and general manager of the Public Works Company.

Graham was also affiliated with the Bangor & Northern which had been reorganized from the Penobscot Central Railroad. (In 1907 Graham took an active part in the consolidation which resulted in the extensive Lewiston, Augusta & Waterville Street Railway of which he served as president).

Development of both the street railways and the power company in Bangor may fully be credited to John R. Graham. He was remembered as a good employer, reportedly learning the names of each of those working for the company.

Although a well-known figure around Bangor, he once boarded a street car on which a new conductor was making his initial trips. Having been impressed with the need for collecting a cash fare or viewing a pass for each and every rider, the conductor failed to recognize Graham who explained that he was the president of the company and seldom bothered to carry a pass.

The new conductor repeated the instructions he had received from the company and insisted upon either viewing a pass or receiving a cash fare—one or the other! Whereupon, the president of the company, without further argument, produced his nickel fare.

At the time of the consolidation of April 1, 1905, the various electric light companies were showing meager returns and the street railways were accounting for over 50 per cent of the earnings of the several companies managed by the Public Works Company. General use of electricity for lighting and power was just coming into acceptance and the transportation department was a vital part of the organization. It was Graham himself who was later to recall: "First came the street railway lines, then the transmission lines."

As of April 1, 1905, the combined roster of the

BANGOR LIBRARY was one of the buildings destroyed in the 1911 conflagration that gutted the other buildings also shown in this circa 1910 view from the State Street bridge over the Kenduskeag. Trolley in distance is turning at Harlow Street.

new operation reported a total of 25 closed cars and 24 open cars, 3 work cars, 6 snow plows, and one "other" car. Although many replacements had been made in the original rolling stock of the Bangor Street Railway, there still remained a few of the older cars.

The following year—1906—the cars of the Bangor & Northern Railway were acquired when that company was merged into the larger system as the Charleston Division on February 1. The two large open cars disappeared from the roster at that time, their disposition unknown. The two large 35-ft. closed cars, after a short trial run on the Brewer Division, were sold to the Waterville system.

Acquisition of the Bangor & Northern added some 28 miles to the Bangor operation. Under the management of the Bangor Railway & Electric Company, this line commenced to receive the attention it so badly needed, with the track being rehabilitated throughout with new ballast and rail bonds.

Power was supplied from the Veazie hydro plant and some $30,000 was spent to improve the supply with an addition to the Park Street substation to make room for two new 500 Kw rotary converters which reduced current losses over the lines by about 20%. A rotary substation was built at Kenduskeag Village and considerable money was spent improving Riverside Park on the Hampden line.

On June 1, 1906, transfer privileges were extended to the Charleston Division with free transfers issued on the local lines covering the first fare zone on the Charleston run.

Further improvements on the Charleston Division were announced June 15. These included an increase to seven daily round trips through to Charleston, and hourly service to North Bangor and Kenduskeag Village. Extra cars also were furnished to meet all passenger trains of the Northern Maine Seaport Railroad, a subsidiary of the Bangor & Aroostook Railroad, at North Bangor. Due to a union controversy, the Maine Central Railroad would not handle passenger trains of the Bangor & Aroostook directly into Bangor.

Extra cars also made connections with arrivals of the Eastern Steamship Company. The trolley company enjoyed a considerable baggage and express business from the steamship wharf to the various hotels of the city.

In conjunction with the newly-opened Northern Maine Seaport Railroad, special excursion trips were offered out of Bangor and from both East Corinth and Charleston by electric car to Seaport Junction, thence over the new steam road to Stockton Springs and Searsport. A further arrangement permitted the public to procure through tickets to any point on the Bangor & Aroostook at the street railway's waiting room in Market Square, using the electric road between Bangor and Seaport Junction.

In an attempt to develop the agricultural economy of the area served by the Charleston Division, the Bangor Railway & Electric Company established a "model farm" close to the Six Mile Falls carbarn to demonstrate modern techniques in farming. This was done in conjunction with experts from the State College in Orono. The company also built a number of potato storage houses along the route to serve as collection centers for this important crop.

The new and modern "car stable," as it was termed, was built in the approximate location of the original carbarn on lower Main Street, but set at right angles to the original one. Opened in 1906, it was claimed as the first use of reinforced concrete for this type of structure. The new building had ample repair facilities for all types of work including heavy repairs,

POST CARD VIEW of Car No. 14 (Brill-built in 1903) at the junction of Hammond and Union Streets, Bangor, about 1906.

which up to this time had been handled by the Union Iron Works of Bangor

In June 1906, the Eastern Traction Company crossed the Bangor horizon for a brief moment, proposing to construct an electric line from Bangor to Dexter, a distance of about 40 miles. It would have left Bangor at a point near Main and Buck Streets, passed along Buck Street to Hammond, through Hammond Street, Cooper Road, Fuller and Clark Roads to the town of Levant, thence through South Levant, following Havelock and Stetson Roads to Stetson Village and Exeter, passing through West Garland near Puffer Pond into Dexter.

This new electric railway project was tied in with a new hydro station being constructed at Milford, a project backed by the A. B. Leach & Company.

Perhaps to forestall encroachment of a possible competitor, President Graham quickly announced that his company had already surveyed a route from Charleston to Dover, and that they were considering other extensions. However, neither the Dover line nor that of the Eastern Traction was ever built.

The new Bangor Railway & Electric Company management announced plans for replacing a mile of the old, light rail annually—a program it carried out until all of Bangor's trackage was of first quality, including the suburban lines. Rail of 70 and 90-pound weight was used in this project.

The Main Street line was completely double-tracked as far as the "Tin Bridge" as was the State Street line as far as Otis Street. Union Street was also double-tracked from Main to Hammond Street.

During 1907 the company purchased four single truck 10-bench open cars, numbering them 1, 3, 5 and 7, and two single truck closed cars numbered 2 and 8, all from the Brill Company. These latter two were replacements for older cars still on the property, having hand-operated brake wheels instead of the conventional goose-neck brake handles, making them unpopular with the carmen.

The same year, one double truck semi-convertible was acquired for the Hampden line and numbered 6.

By 1908 all of the older cars had been disposed of and all closed cars were of Brill manufacture. With the exception of a few cars purchased later from Laconia, all other cars came from Brill or its subsidiaries, American Car or Wason.

Bridges were ever a problem to the Bangor street railway system. At the time of consolidation in 1905, the Brewer Division remained physically separated, unable to gain a crossing of the Penobscot River. The cities of Bangor and Brewer had joined forces to take over ownership of the ancient wooden toll span following the 1902 freshet which had washed away one section of the structure. An iron center span was built by the municipalities, with a small steam launch connecting the two cities in the interim. The remaining portion of the bridge was not suitable for electric cars, however.

The long wooden double-barrelled covered bridge across the Stillwater River at Orono was also cause for concern, especially after the heavy semi-convertible cars were placed on the Old Town run in 1903. Final decision as to the safety of the span was left to the Orono town fathers who were slow in making judgment. Accordingly, at the request of the street railway management, the Maine Railroad Commissioners had the bridge examined by a bridge engineer.

The span was condemned for use by electric cars in October 1907, as the chords and beams were badly

"NEW" BANGOR CARBARN on lower Main Street, opened in 1906 as part of the new management's upgrading of facilities.

out of line. Under orders from the Railroad Commission, the bridge was substantially rebuilt, with the Town of Orono contributing the sum of $2,500 and the street railway $6,000.

Trolley traffic over the span was resumed in March, 1908. In 1912 the wooden bridge was replaced by a steel structure, with the town contributing 40% and the street railway the remainder.

The two long wooden covered bridges within the city of Bangor over which the Charleston line operated apparently gave little trouble through the years, even though long and heavy electric freight trains passed over them daily.

The wooden bridge at South Brewer over the Segeunkedunk Stream was replaced by a concrete span in 1909 in conjunction with the city's street rebuilding program which was to place the trolley line in the center of the street throughout the length of Main Street.

The two municipal bridges over the Kenduskeag Stream in downtown Bangor were badly damaged in the conflagration of 1911 and required substantial rebuilding.

The bridge at Six Mile Falls was washed out by a flood in the spring of 1920. On the Hampden line the old wooden span was replaced by a modern highway-railway bridge in 1925.

In keeping with the improvements being made throughout the system, the Bangor Railway & Electric Company extended its Hammond Street line from Fourteenth Street to Seventeenth Street in 1908. A one-mile extension of the Hampden line to Dorothea Dix Park, a popular picnic area, opened November 8, 1913. On September 28, 1914, electric cars commenced operation over the newly-completed steel bridge over the Penobscot River between Bangor and Brewer—the first time that the Brewer Division had been linked with the rest of the system.

The Westland Avenue extension was the last major building job of the Bangor system. This opened in 1922, bringing together the outer ends of the Hammond Street and the Ohio Street lines, forming a loop around which cars ran in both directions. When this was completed, the new Westland Avenue loop was combined with the State-Garland loop. The Center Street cars were then routed along Main Street, terminating at the "Tin Bridge."

Hampden, Old Town and Brewer cars turned in downtown Bangor via State, Central and Exchange Streets. The Charleston cars had their terminal on Broad Street.

1902 FRESHET washed away center span and approach to Bangor-Brewer covered bridge and railroad span in foreground.

The great Bangor fire which broke out about 4 p. m. on Sunday, April 30, 1911, destroyed much of the heart of the business section. It claimed the general offices of the Bangor Railway & Electric Company as well as its Park Street substation. The Bangor Public Library with its 300,000 volumes was a complete ruin as were the rooms of the Bangor Historical Society. The Bangor Railway & Electric Company immediately announced plans to rebuild on a finer scale and offered aid to all who had suffered loss.

Two monitor roof, double truck semi-convertible cars were purchased during 1910 for the Old Town line (Nos. 80 and 82) while in 1911 a double truck closed car (No. 42) was purchased for the Hampden line. In 1913 three additional double truck semi-convertible cars were acquired (Nos. 84, 86 and 88). These were built by the Wason Manufacturing Company, a subsidiary of Brill. They had arched roofs and set the pattern for rolling stock on the Old Town line thereafter.

Two similar cars arrived from the same source in 1914 (Nos. 90 and 92) In 1916 the last of this series was received (Nos. 94 and 96). These final two cars were one window longer than previous equipment and initially were fitted with HL controls for multiple-unit operation, a system other Maine roads were experimenting with. The feasibility of two-car trains on the Old Town line did not prove itself, as the two cars were soon rebuilt for single car operation.

The 25-year franchise granted to the old Bangor Street Railway expired in 1913 and the company was engaged in a typical lengthy joust with the city fathers regarding its renewal. The company objected to the wording of a city council order passed on August 2, 1912, on the grounds that it was ambiguous; that it named the Bangor Street Railway as the party of interest, although the same had long since ceased to exist as a corporation.

The order had also made the crossing of the new bridge to Brewer a part of the original agreement. It was not until late in the year that a suitable compromise was worked out, though the tax on gross profits of street railway operation was retained.

The year 1914 saw the Old Town Division completely equipped with Chapman automatic block signals as was the Charleston Division as far as Buckley's Siding. The remainder of the Charleston Division was equipped with these protective devices the following year. Within a short time, all of the Bangor system was so covered.

After a freight car rolled free from a siding on the Charleston line one night, resulting in a crash involving an open car, the company installed 13 sets of standard derailers at all freight sidings and spurs in 1915.

The arrival of the new semi-convertible cars in 1916 introduced the prepayment system of fare collection to Bangor. All closed cars were rebuilt for this advanced method of collecting fares. Previously, passengers boarding cars would find a seat, after which the conductor would walk forward to pick up the fare. With the prepayment, or "pay-as-you-enter" system, passengers paid their fares upon boarding, permitting the conductor to remain at his station on the rear platform. Rooke fare registers were adopted as a means of keeping tally on the fares.

The Bangor system remained more or less free of the spectacular trolley wrecks which haunted some roads. A check of the Railroad Commissioners' reports reveals no untoward disaster throughout the years. One former street car man has suggested it was because the Bangor cars moved so slowly that no serious accident could occur! Which must be taken with a grain of salt.

In 1911 car No. 42 did run wild down Park Street Hill, leaving the rails at the intersection of State and

BANGOR-BREWER SPAN with steel center section and approach after its 1902 rebuilding, but still unsuitable for car tracks.

JOHN R. GRAHAM, 1844-1915.

Exchange Streets and plunging into the cellar hole of a building which had been destroyed by the conflagration a short time previously. Both carmen were hurt in this crash. The only passenger, a police officer dead-heading to the stationhouse, made a hasty escape from the rear platform. The car was a total loss and was replaced by another of the same number.

Another runaway car in 1913 raced down Hammond Street Hill, left the rails and came to a stop just inches from crashing through the great doors of Hose Three's firehouse. No injuries were reported.

John R. Graham died August 24, 1915. He was succeeded as president of the Bangor Railway & Electric Company by Erastus C. Ryder who continued in that office until 1920. He was replaced by Edward M. Graham, son of John Graham, who served from 1921 until 1958 when he was named chairman of the board of the Bangor Hydro-Electric Company.

Riverside Park, which had often seen as many as a dozen electric cars hauling merrymakers, began to lose favor with the public with the changing times and the trend away from trolley parks. The company had taken delivery of three double truck, steam coach roof open cars from the Laconia Car Company in 1912 to aid in handling the resort-bound traffic.

They were the last open cars purchased by the Bangor system and among the last open cars to be built for a North American street railway. Despite the new cars and the maintenance of Riverside Park at a high level, 1916 proved to be the final year of its operation and its spur track was removed the following spring.

The trend nationwide was toward a low-step, prepayment car which would accept a crowd of passengers quickly. The Laconia Car Company had experimented with a 4-wheel center entrance car supposedly incorporating all of these desirable features, and in 1916 the Bangor Railway & Electric Company took delivery of three of this type (Nos. 8, 10 and 12).

In Bangor these cars were dubbed "submarines" and referred to as the "U-8, U-10 and U-12." The cars reportedly were good in snow, but the Radiax-type truck with its form of floating axle, was said to have been difficult to re-rail—and the cars seemed to jump the track fairly frequently. (The Lewiston, Maine, system also had a group of similar cars).

The advent of the one-man car followed closely upon the development of these center entrance types which necessitated two-man operation. Thus the cars

CENTER ENTRANCE CAR NO. 10 aboard a steam railroad flat car at the Laconia Car Company plant for shipment to Bangor Railway & Electric, 1916.

CONTRAST OF THE SEASONS in Bangor (page opposite). Open car No. 21 was built by Newburyport in 1890 and later rebuilt by Bangor Street Railway with vestibules and brake wheels instead of handles, as were Nos. 17 and 19 also. A winter scene shows No. 20 on Main Street near the fairgrounds. This was the second car No. 20, built in 1903.

were soon obsolete and in 1920 they were sold to a Massachusetts equipment broker at a considerable loss.

The Bangor system had also acquired a double truck center entrance trailer numbered 200 which was converted into a motor car and renumbered 98—but the day of the two-man trolley car was rapidly coming to a close.

Along with the carmen of the Portland and Lewiston systems, the Bangor motormen and conductors had been working toward the organization of a union and affiliation with the national brotherhood.

In order to enforce their demands, a strike was voted and on August 26, 1916, all electric cars were returned to the carbarns at 9 o'clock in the morning. The usual charges and counter-charges were issued by the company and the carmen alike, with special sessions of the city council endeavoring to conciliate the matter.

The Bangor police department closed all saloons and raided a few which did not heed its admonition. Rumors flew about Bangor for two days of 50 strikebreakers being imported from New York City to take over operation of the cars. (This had been done in Portland.)

For the two-day period, the newspapers reported that these worthies were being held at Newport, 35 miles away. The strike-breakers never reached Bangor. Which may have been just as well! With the aid of supervisory personnel and non-union carmen, some semblance of service was given throughout the strike, but most patrons shunned the cars. Only minor disturbances were reported, although at Hampden one car was pelted with over-ripe fruit.

Like most street railway strikes of the period, this one came to a predictable end, with the company recognizing the union. The carmen, meeting in downtown Bangor, formed a procession and paraded back to the carhouse to commence their runs.

World War I lent an impetus to the freight and express operations on the street railways throughout

New England and Bangor was no exception. With the steam railroad facilities taxed to the limit, more and more of this traffic was routed via the electric lines.

The Bangor system became the third largest electric line carrier of freight in the Pine Tree State, topped only by the Lewiston, Augusta & Waterville Street Railway and the Atlantic Shore Railway.

The old Penobscot Central route, which had become the Charleston Division of the Bangor Railway & Electric Company, was primarily a freight line. Two regular daily freight and express trips were scheduled, with extra trains to handle carload freight as required.

Express motors were frequently double-headed on this division with as many as 10 or more standard steam railroad freight cars making up the consist. Freight originated at the Eastern Steamship Company's wharf where the electric railway had a convenient freight shed.

There was an interchange track in Bangor with the Maine Central Railroad at Broad and Front Streets and one with the Bangor & Aroostook Railroad at North Bangor. Both steam roads interchanged cars with the electric line.

Several grocery and provision wholesale houses located along Broad Street in Bangor depended upon the electric road to spot refrigerator and other cars arriving on the Maine Central in front of their doors.

A third interchange was established on the Hampden line near the "Tin Bridge" with the Maine Central to serve several prosperous industries on that line, which included a lumber yard and a cement block plant.

On June 24, 1918, freight and express service commenced on the Old Town Division, with one regular daily round trip out of Bangor. An interchange was established with the Maine Central in Veazie to handle carload shipments.

At the University of Maine in Orono, a spur track was built into the steam plant to handle carload coal and a small freight shed was located nearby. Another

13-BENCH OPEN CAR No. 9 on the Hampden line was one of three large opens purchased in 1912 for Riverside Park traffic.

ON THE CHARLESTON LINE—Above, No. 34 is at East Corinth; below, same car is seen in Kenduskeag Village; circa 1910.

freight shed was located in Old Town near Main Street and Stillwater Avenue.

To boost power on the Charleston line for heavier freight business, the company installed a new 300 KW rotary converter at the East Corinth freight house in 1917.

A total of 94,353 car miles were reported by the freight department for the year ending June 30, 1919, and freight income for that period was $52,644.81, a not inconsiderable sum in those days.

Conditions during the First World War in Bangor were much the same as those throughout the nation, with inflation pushing up the price of coal, iron, steel, copper, wages and all other items pertinent to street railway operation.

Also, there was a marked decrease in the number of riders with many of the male citizens in the armed services and a slowing down of many normal public and social functions. The 1918 influenza epidemic took its toll, reportedly accounting for a temporary 20% reduction in riding when the public was urged to stay away from crowds and avoid all unnecessary contacts with others.

Accordingly, the Bangor Railway & Electric Company followed the country-wide pattern of gradually increasing fares, first to 6 cents, then to 7 cents and eventually to 8 cents for a basic ride.

Passenger receipts for the 1919 year ending June 30th, amounted to $432,683.64. Operating expenses, however, were outstripping income—a familiar plight in the street railway industry.

During the early months of 1920, there occurred what has ever since been referred to as the "Blizzard of the Century" in the State of Maine—snowstorms which completely tied up both steam and electric rail lines for days at a time. One motorman described fighting his way through to Old Town in the storm and not being able to make his return run for 10 days!

A holiday was proclaimed at the University of Maine in Orono with every able bodied male student turning out to aid in digging out the trolley line.

In contrast, the year 1920 saw the final regular operation of the open cars in Bangor. This made it possible to close the carbarn on State Street which had been used for a number of years for storage of out-of-season cars. This barn had been built by the Bangor, Orono & Old Town Railway in 1895.

Another bad winter—that of 1922-23—saw a serious fire threatening to wipe out the built-up section of Kenduskeag Village. Called upon for aid, the Bangor

INTERIOR OF BIRNEY CAR NO. 20—The clean lines and the wooden seats were a feature of most of the cars of this type.

Fire Department was powerless to buck the drifts of snow which were reported to be six to eight feet deep across the highway.

Only the street railway, which had labored to keep its tracks open with its rotary plow, offered a chance of reaching the stricken community. Providing flat cars, the street railway soon had Bangor's fire-fighting force loaded and on the way behind two double-headed freight motors led by the rotary plow. They arrived in time to assist in halting the conflagration.

The fall of 1918 saw the arrival of the first one-man Birney "Safety Cars" in the Queen City, when the company took delivery of three of these single truck cars from the American Car Company, a Brill subsidiary. The cars were given numbers 20, 22 and 24.

Features of this new rolling stock included interlocked brake and power control which placed stress on simplicity of operation and safety. With one motion, the "operator"—he would no longer be called "motorman"—could shut off his power, apply the brakes, sand the rails and open the doors.

Low power consumption and a high rate of acceleration was the street railway industry's answer to the public's increasing interest in the automobile; thousands of Birney cars were put into service throughout the nation. Although they never quite fulfilled all of the claims made for them, they served Bangor faithfully and well for some 27 years.

Twelve additional Birney cars, Nos. 44 through 66 (even numbers) were received from the American Car Company during 1919, replacing the majority of the older single truck closed cars in use on the local runs. Two more cars of the same type were received in 1922 from the Wason Company (Nos. 38 and 40).

In 1923 the final single truck Birney car was purchased second hand through an equipment broker (No. 42). This car had been in service on the Concord, Maynard & Hudson (Mass.) Street Railway where it had carried number 200.

With the acceptance of the one-man Birney safety car on the local lines, the Bangor Railway & Electric Company rebuilt its fleet of large, double truck, semi-convertible cars for one-man operation. The older double truck cars built for the Bangor, Orono & Old Town road in 1903, the two combination cars normally used on the Charleston Division and the double truck center entrance car were scrapped at that time.

In rebuilding these cars for one-man operation, the rear door on either side was enclosed and replaced with a window. Full safety controls were installed, along with air-operated doors. Cleveland fare boxes replaced the Rooke hand registers for fare collection.

Six double truck lightweight safety cars arrived in Bangor from the Wason Company during 1922, primarily for the Hampden and Brewer lines. They were numbered 8, 10, 12, 14, 16 and 18.

A seventh car of the same type, but with slight modification, arrived in 1923 (No. 6). Thus, at the time when the company was due for a further financial reshuffle, the Bangor area could boast of a thoroughly modern traction operation.

BANGOR'S FIRST BIRNEY CAR, NO. 20, as it looked about 1935 when photographed on Main Street opposite the carbarn.

Six Mile Falls Bridge . . .

Threatened by a freshet and ice jams following the severe winter of 1920, the Bangor Railway & Electric Co. tried in vain to save the bridge by placing loaded freight cars on the span. They were pulled away when it became apparent that they, too, would be swept into the Kenduskeag Stream. The 1920 photos below show the bridge, first on March 17, as it had stood for many years propped up with trestlework to support freight trains; then as it looked March 30 weighted down with loaded cars; and in the bottom photo on April 7 as it appeared the day after the trestle bents were swept downstream by ice.

NEW SIX MILE FALLS BRIDGE was opened to traffic December 25, 1920. Passenger service in the interim was maintained by the car stranded on the outer end of the line and a boat in which the crew rowed their passengers past the bridge site.

FREIGHT TRAIN on the Charleston line is typified by this two-car consist headed by express motor 106. —From a clipping.

Bangor Hydro-Electric Company

Certain reorganizations in the financial structure of the Bangor Railway & Electric Company resulted when the General Electric Company divested itself of its subsidiary, the Electric Bond & Share Company, in 1924. As a result, the Bangor Hydro-Electric Company was organized June 9, 1924. Stock in this new corporation was exchanged on an equal basis for stock in the Bangor Railway & Electric Company. The new company formally took over operation March 1, 1925.

At that time the Bangor trolley system was operating a total of 58.73 miles of main line track, including the lengthy Charleston line. Rolling stock consisted of 9 double truck semi-convertible cars, 7 double truck safety cars and 18 single truck Birney safety cars. All of the large semi-convertibles had been rebuilt for one-man operation during 1923, with full safety controls, air-operated doors and Cleveland fare boxes.

One single truck Birney car was dropped from the roster in 1926. This was No. 42, the one purchased second hand in 1923. It was scrapped at the Six Mile Falls carhouse where the other older cars also were scrapped.

Three of the double truck safety cars (Nos. 6, 10 and 14) were rebuilt with 35 hp. motors intended for use on the Old Town Division, but they were unable to maintain the scheduled time and were used as rush hour extras as far as Veazie.

No cars were ever purchased by the Bangor Hydro-Electric Company, the reliable semi-convertibles handling the long suburban runs, the double truck safety cars the Hampden and Brewer lines and the single truck safety cars the local Bangor city routes.

When the Maine Central Railroad abandoned trackage through Veazie during 1926, including the former freight interchange connection, the Bangor Hydro-Electric secured the right-of-way and rebuilt a line about one-third of a mile in length to a gravel bank to obtain ballast for track work.

In 1930 a 700-ft. extension off the Hampden line was built to serve the plant of the Hughes Brothers Company near the "Tin Bridge." This was the last track addition by the company.

The 1920s were marked by a movement to build better highways and farmers were acquiring their own trucks to haul their produce to market. Trucking firms

ROTARY PLOW M-6 got frequent workouts in Bangor. Photo opposite page shows it on the Charleston line March 2, 1920.

PLOWS ON STATE STREET February 26, 1920, after one of the big storms of that winter. Even after the weather cleared there was so much snow on the ground that frequent plowing on all lines was necessary to keep rails clear. Photo on page 48 at left shows a Wason 4-wheel shear plow leading express motors 102 and 108 (also fitted with plows) out State Street.

BIRNEY CARS proved their mettle in snow the first winter in Bangor. Here is No. 56 on outer State Street in March 1920.

also were springing up as the highway system was improved and expanded, offering door-to-door service. It forecast the end of trolley freight operations.

The Charleston Division, sustained by the dependable electric freight service and without comparable passenger traffic, fell victim to the changing times. On April 30, 1931, the Charleston Division was abandoned in its entirety.

The rails were cut back to the junction of Harlow and Cumberland Streets in Bangor and the days when double-headed express motors would rumble over the two wooden covered bridges across the Kenduskeag Stream had come to an end.

A private bus service took over to handle the few passengers and the mail over the Charleston route with the discontinuance of electric cars. In 1940 the Bangor Hydro took back this route when it inaugurated the Penobscot Transportation Company in the gradual changeover to bus operation.

Weekly passes were introduced in 1932 with successful results. A one dollar pass covered the initial fare zone and included all of Bangor and Brewer. Another pass covered the second fare zone that included all of the Hampden line and the Old Town Division as far as the University of Maine. A third pass covered the entire system through to Great Works.

These passes were transferable and they tended to speed up service as it reduced time required to make change and eliminated the need for transfers. The passes were a real transportation bargain.

In 1939 the price of these passes was reduced and one selling for a dollar covered the first two fare zones. A shoppers' pass was also available for 50 cents, good between 10 a. m. and 4 p. m. on weekdays, after 6 in the evening and all day Sunday. Low-cost student passes also were provided.

Following the practice of many street railways of the period, Bangor elected to brighten up its rolling stock in 1934. As the cars rolled out of the paint shop following their annual overhaul, they sported a yellow hue rather than the dark green and cream of former days. They had come full cycle, as the first electric cars in Bangor had likewise been painted yellow with cream trim.

Lettering along the sides advertised the weekly passes, while the Bangor Hydro-Electric Company monogram appeared on each car. Lighter colors helped to make the cars more visible, especially at night, tending to reduce accidents.

The Public Utilities Holding Act of 1935 brought about further adjustments in the corporate structure of the Bangor Hydro-Electric Company, but this had no effect upon the street railway operations.

It might be recorded that in 1935 the street railway was indirectly influential in bringing about the complete motorization of the fire department of the City of Old Town. In responding to an alarm of fire, the horse drawing the city's last horse-drawn hose rig slipped on the car rails, breaking its leg. The animal

BIRNEY CARS on the Hammond Street-Westland Avenue loop met on a turnout in the open country which in 1939 became the site of Dow Airfield of the U. S. Air Force. In upper photo on the opposite page, No. 52 waits on the switch for a meet as Linwood Moody (Maine narrow gauge historian, in white shirt and tie) chats with the operator. In lower view of No. 56 going into the turnout, the open character of the land is evident. Both photos July 15, 1938, by H. T. Crittenden, E. Bond collection.

"VEAZIE" EXTRA—No. 12 lightweight awaits departure from the carbarn as a rush hour turnback on the Old Town line.

was disposed of and the hose wagon was replaced with a motor truck

Routes of the Bangor cars during the 1930s and until the end of operations included the HIGHLANDS and the HAMMOND STREET lines which ran in opposing directions around the Westland Avenue loop at one side of the city and also in opposing directions in making the GARLAND STREET and the STATE STREET runs at the other end.

The CENTER STREET line looped at one end and terminated at the "Tin Bridge" on the MAIN STREET line at the other end. Other routes included the HAMPDEN, the BREWER and the OLD TOWN lines which made the loop downtown for the return run. There was no longer a CHARLESTON line after 1931.

Fifteen- and 20-minute headway was in effect on local city runs and to Brewer, with half-hourly service to Old Town. The Hampden line was served by two cars with a 40-minute headway.

In contrast with most street railways which were drastically curtailing service—if not abandoning operations altogether—the Bangor Hydro in 1939 issued a new schedule with improved headways.

Thirty-minute headway was provided on the Hampden line along with additional rush hour cars both morning and night on the city lines. Bangor not only improved service, but cut the price of the weekly passes!

In keeping with various state highway improvement projects, the Bangor system had reconstructed portions of its lines, but there came a time when this became economically unfeasible. Accordingly, a half mile of the outer end of the Hampden line was cut back in late 1939 when state highway reconstruction called for track relocation.

This same year, as the Federal government began to develop Dow Air Field, the Westland Avenue track had to be abandoned, being in the way of the enlargement of the flying field. This trackage tied together the Hammond Street and the Highlands lines.

The Hammond Street line was cut back to the junction of Westland Avenue, while the route on Ohio Street to the Highlands was terminated at the corner of Westland Avenue just beyond Mt. Pleasant Cemetery. The turnouts on Ohio Street at the cemetery and on Hammond Street were removed.

Operations over the remainder of the Hampden line came to a close July 27, 1940, again as a result of further highway reconstruction. Double truck safety car No. 10 made the final run with operator Edgar W. Bille leaving Bangor at 11 p. m.

On board this last run to Hampden was company president Edward M. Graham, superintendent Charles H. Johnson and other officials. Both Graham and Johnson took over the controls on portions of the run.

Superintendent Johnson had operated the first car into Hampden when the original portion of the road was opened as the Bangor, Hampden & Winterport Railway in 1896. President Graham treated all hands to ice cream sodas at Hampden as impromptu rites for the demise of street railway service were held.

With the abandonment of the Hampden line, the Penobscot Transportation Company, a newly-organized subsidiary of the Bangor Hydro-Electric Company, commenced the operation of three White buses the following morning between Market Square and Hampden. These vehicles ran express as far as the "Tin Bridge" in both directions.

The Penobscot Transportation Company took over operation of the transportation department of the

HAMMOND STREET CARS were cut back to this point on Hammond after 1939. Note that track has been removed going around corner onto Westland Avenue where it went through the fields to Ohio Street. —Photo by S. D. Maguire, May 1944.

Bangor Hydro-Electric Company in 1940. A final color scheme soon appeared, with the trolley cars carrying a wide, dark red stripe around the belt rail and with the front numbers being painted on the letterboard above the front window, which matched the paint scheme of the new buses.

That same year—1940—semi-convertible cars Nos. 80 and 92 were scrapped.

State highway reconstruction continued and on March 29, 1941, the lines to Brewer and Old Town were abandoned. Handling the controls of the last car to Brewer was Superintendent Johnson who had operated the first car over the bridge between the two cities in 1914. With him as honorary running mate was the conductor of that first trip over the Penobscot, Charles Smith, well into his 80s and long in retirement.

The final run from Old Town did not lay up at the carhouse until 1:42 a. m. the following morning. Buses

of the Penobscot Transportation Company took over both of these runs that morning.

At the beginning, the "modern" motor vehicles left downtown Bangor via State Street hill rather than use the more circuitous route via Exchange, Washington and Oak Streets. Following several accidents on the icy hill, the buses were rerouted along the old trolley route.

It had been the intention of the company to "phase out" the remaining trolley operations by the end of 1943, but the acute shortages brought on by World War II held up this plan, with the faithful Birney cars providing service on the local lines. The double truck semi-convertible cars were all scrapped in 1942.

The seven double truck safety cars, no longer required, were sold to the Johnstown (Penna.) Traction Company in 1942, where they were renumbered 305 through 311.

All but No. 311 were scrapped by that company in

ON THE OLD TOWN LINE—Photos taken by H. T. Crittenden, July 15, 1938, were loaned from collection of **Edward Bond**.

LAST RUN—President Graham of Bangor Hydro-Electric at controls of No. 40, above. He stands in doorway as Operator Thomas Davis poses for photo on State Street, Bangor, as No. 40 was making a final circuit of the city trolley lines.

1947 at Johnstown, but No. 311 remained in service to make one of the final runs of that company in 1961— the last small city street railway operation in the United States.

No. 311 has since been acquired by the Rock Hill Furnace, Penna., railroad museum and is in daily service during the tourist season.

With the end of the war bringing about a lessening of restrictions, the street railway service in Bangor came to an end December 31, 1945.

A special trip covering all remaining routes and trackage with car No. 40 was made with company officials and veteran employees. Leaving the carbarn at 3 p. m. with Operator Thomas Davis at the controls, the car ran over every route, returning to the barn at 4:10 p. m.

Following this, the party made its way to the Park Street substation where at 4:26 p. m. President Graham personally pulled the switch cutting off for all time the power to the street railway lines.

Having been the first electric street railway in the State of Maine, the Bangor system came close to being the last. At the time trolley service ended in the Queen City, only the York Utilities Company was in operation over its 3-mile line between Sanford and Springvale. Passenger service there continued until 1947 and trolley freight operation until 1949 when diesels took over.

Out of Presque Isle, the Aroostook Valley Railroad in 1945 was still operating one daily passenger interurban run for school children. Freight operations on this road had already been dieselized and with the coming of spring of 1946 all trolley operations on the road ceased.

WINTER 1920—Trolley lines all over New England experienced the worst winter operating conditions that year. Bangor, likewise had its problems. Dump car M-12 helps remove the ice on State Street after men with pickaxes break it into pieces.

BANGOR STREET RAILWAY
CAR ROSTER 1889-1905

Car No.	Type of Car	Builder	Year Built	Notes
10	16-ft. box	Newburyport	1888	
11	16-ft. box	Newburyport	1888	
12	16-ft. box	Newburyport	1888	First car over the road.
13	16-ft. box	Newburyport	1888	
14	8-bench open	Newburyport	1889	
15	8-bench open	Newburyport	1889	
16	8-bench open	Newburyport	1889	
17	8-bench open	Newburyport	1889	
18	18-ft. box	Newburyport	1889	
19	18-ft. box	Newburyport	1890	There is evidence that
20	18-ft. box	Newburyport	1890	certain of these 1890
21	18-ft. box	Newburyport	1890	cars were built for the
22	8-bench open	Newburyport	1890	Newburyport Car Co.
23	8-bench open	Newburyport	1890	by the Ellis Car Co. of
24	8-bench open	Newburyport	1890	Amesbury, Mass., but
25	8-bench open	Newburyport	1890	which ones is not ascer-
26	8-bench open	Newburyport	1890	tainable. All were re-
27	8-bench open	Newburyport	1890	ferred to as "Newbury-
28	8-bench open	Newburyport	1890	port" cars.
29	8-bench open	Newburyport	1890	
30	18-ft. box	Newburyport	1890	
31	8-bench open	Newburyport	1890	
32	8-bench open	Newburyport	1890	
33	8-bench open	Newburyport	1890	
34	18-ft. box	Newburyport	1890	
35	18-ft. box	Newburyport	1890	
36	18-ft. box	Newburyport	1890	
37	18-ft. box	Newburyport	1890	
38	18-ft. box	Newburyport	1890	
39	18-ft. box	Newburyport	1890	
40	Snow plow	Dorner & Dutton	1889	Not motorized the first winter.

At the time of the 1905 consolidation, Bangor Street Railway reported a total of 14 box cars, 17 open cars, 3 snow plows and 2 electric automobiles.

Car replacements by years are listed below. Absence of records due to total destruction of the Bangor Railway & Electric Compay offices in Bangor's Great Fire of 1911 has made accurate research impossible. However, company policy was to give a new car the number of the one it replaced and this practice apparently was followed throughout the company's history.

1893   Five box cars retired, presumably of the earliest type.

1894   One 18-ft. box car purchased.

1895   Two 16-ft. ex-horse cars purchased from West End Street Railway of Boston, Nos. 1759 and 2169. One "band" car purchased second-hand (single truck express car).

1896   Four 16-ft. motorized ex-horse cars purchased from West End Street Railway of Boston, Nos. 1380, 1388, 1438 and 1489.

1897   One box car scrapped; one open car rebuilt for work service.

1898   One box car scrapped.

1899   One open car purchased; one ex-horse car to Penobscot Central.

1901   Two box cars and two open cars scrapped.

1903   Nos. 41, 16, 18, 20, 22, 24 and 26, 18-ft. box cars purchased from Brill.

1904   Four 10-bench opens transferred from Bangor, Orono & Old Town and equipped with maximum traction trucks.

ORIGINAL SNOW PLOW No. 40 after being motorized.

BANGOR RAILWAY & ELECTRIC COMPANY
CAR ROSTER 1905 - 1924

Car No.	Type of Car	Builder	Year Built	Trucks	Motors	Control	Notes
STANDARD CLOSED CARS							
2	18-ft. box	Newburyport	1890				Ex-Bangor Street Railway
2	20-ft. box	Brill	1907	Brill 21E	2-GE80		
4	18-ft. box	Newburyport	1890				Ex-Bangor Street Railway
6	18-ft. box	Newburyport	1890				Ex-Bangor Street Railway
6	25-ft. 4-in. box	Laconia	1907	Brill 22E	2-WH306	K-36G	
8	18-ft. box	Newburyport	1890				Ex-Bangor Street Railway
8	20-ft. box	Brill	1907	Brill 21E	2-GE80	K-10	
10	18-ft. box	Newburyport	1890				Ex-Bangor Street Railway
12	18-ft. box	Brill	1894				Ex-Bangor Street Railway
14	18-ft. box	Brill	1902	Brill 21E	2-WH307	K-36	
16	18-ft. box	Brill	1902	Brill 21E	2-WH307	K-36	
18	18-ft. box	Brill	1903	Brill 21E	2-WH307	K-36J	
20	18-ft. box	Brill	1903	Brill 21E	2-GE70	K-36J	
22	18-ft. box	Brill	1903	Brill 21E	2-GE67	K-10	
24	18-ft. box	Brill	1903	Brill 21E	2-GE67	K-10	
26	18-ft. box	Brill	1903	Brill 21E	2-GE67	K-10	
28	20-ft. box	Brill	1906	Brill 21E	2-GE80	K-10	
30	20-ft. box	Brill	1906	Brill 21E	2-GE80	K-10	
32	28-ft. combine	Brill	1906	Baldwin	4-GE80	K-28	
34	28-ft. combine	Brill	1906	Baldwin	4-GE80	K-28B	
36	20-ft. box	Brill	1897	Brill 21E	2-WH307	K-36	Ex-Bangor, Hampden & Wint'p't
38	20-ft. box	Brill	1897	Brill 21E	2-WH307	K-36G	Ex-Bangor, Hampden & Wint'p't
40	20-ft. box	Brill	1897	Brill 21E	2-GE80	K-10	Ex-Bangor, Hampden & Wint'p't
42	20-ft. box	Brill	1897				Wrecked 1911
42	25-ft. semi-conv.	Laconia	1911	Brill 27G	4-GE80	K-28J	
SEMI-CONVERTIBLE CARS							
68	28-ft. semi	Brill	1902	Brill 27G	4-GE70	K-28	Ex-Bangor, Orono & Old Town
70	28-ft. semi	Brill	1902	Brill 27G	4-GE70	K-28A	Ex-Bangor, Orono & Old Town
72	28-ft. semi	Brill	1902	Brill 27G	4-GE70	K-28A	Ex-Bangor, Orono & Old Town
74	28-ft. semi	Brill	1902	Brill 27G	4-GE70	K-28A	Ex-Bangor, Orono & Old Town
76	28-ft. semi	Brill	1902	Brill 27G	4-GE70	K-28A	Ex-Bangor, Orono & Old Town
78	28-ft. semi	Brill	1903	Brill 27G	4-GE70	K-28A	Ex-Bangor, Orono & Old Town
80	30-ft. 8-in. semi	Brill	1910	Brill 27MCB	4-GE80	K-28	Later WH307 motors
82	30-ft. 8-in. semi	Brill	1910	Brill 27MCB	4-GE80	K-28B	
84	30-ft. 10-in. semi	Wason	1913	Brill 27MCB	4-WH306	K-35G	
86	30-ft. 10-in. semi	Wason	1913	Brill 27MCB	4-WH306	K-35G	
88	30-ft. 10-in. semi	Wason	1913	Brill 27MCB	4-WH306	K-35G	
90	30-ft. 8-in. semi	Wason	1914	Brill 27MCB	4-GE201	K-35G	
92	30-ft. 8-in. semi	Wason	1914	Brill 27MCB	4-GE201	K-35G	
94	33-ft. 4-in. semi	Wason	1916	Brill 27MCB	4-WH306	HL-15B	Later K-35G control
96	33-ft. 4-in. semi	Wason	1916	Brill 27MCB	4-WH305	HL-15B	Later K-35G control
CENTER ENTRANCE CARS							
8	23-ft. 9-in. c. en.	Laconia	1916	Halsey	2-WH532	K-36J	Sold 1920
10	23-ft. 9-in. c. en.	Laconia	1916	Halsey	2-WH532	K-36J	Sold 1920
12	23-ft. 9-in. c. en.	Laconia	1916	Halsey	2-WH532	K-36J	Sold 1920
200	35-ft. 8½-in. c. en.	Brill	1917	Brill 77E	Trailer		No. 200 converted to motor car
98	35-ft. 8½-in. c. en.						No. 98 in 1919 or 1920.

CENTER ENTRANCE CAR No. 200 from a Brill builder's photo.

BANGOR RAILWAY & ELECTRIC COMPANY
CAR ROSTER 1905 - 1924

Car No.	Type of Car	Builder	Year Built	Trucks	Motors	Control	Notes
BIRNEY CARS							
20	Birney safety	American	1918	Brill 79M1B	2-GE258	K-10	
22	Birney safety	American	1918	Brill 79M1B	2-GE258	K-10	
24	Birney safety	American	1918	Brill 79M1B	2-GE258	K-10	
38	Birney safety	Wason	1922	Brill 79E1	2-GE258	K-63	
40	Birney safety	Wason	1922	Brill 79E1	2-GE258	K-63	
42	Birney safety	American	1918	Brill 78M1F	2-WH506	K-63	
44	Birney safety	American	1919	Brill 78M1F	2-GE258	K-63	
46	Birney safety	American	1919	Brill 78M1F	2-GE258	K-63	
48	Birney safety	American	1919	Brill 78M1F	2-GE258	K-63	
50	Birney safety	American	1919	Brill 78M1F	2-GE258	K-63	
52	Birney safety	American	1919	Brill 78M1F	2-GE258	K-63	
54	Birney safety	American	1919	Brill 78M1F	2-GE258	K-63	
56	Birney safety	American	1919	Brill 78M1F	2-GE258	K-63	
58	Birney safety	American	1919	Brill 78M1F	2-GE258	K-63	
60	Birney safety	American	1919	Brill 78M1F	2-GE258	K-63	
62	Birney safety	American	1919	Brill 78M1F	2-GE258	K-63	
64	Birney safety	American	1919	Brill 78M1F	2-GE258	K-63	
66	Birney safety	American	1919	Brill 78M1F	2-GE258	K-63	
DOUBLE TRUCK SAFETY CARS							
6	29-ft. 6-in. safety	Wason	1921	Brill 77E1	4-GE258	K-35	Later GE265 motors
8	29-ft. 6-in. safety	Wason	1921	Brill 77E1	4-GE258	K-35	
10	29-ft. 6-in. safety	Wason	1921	Brill 77E1	4-GE258	K-35	Later GE265 motors
12	29-ft. 6-in. safety	Wason	1921	Brill 77E1	4-GE258	K-35	
14	29-ft. 6-in. safety	Wason	1921	Brill 77E1	4-GE258	K-35	Later GE265 motors
16	29-ft. 6-in. safety	Wason	1921	Brill 77E1	4-GE258	K-35	
18	29-ft. 6-in. safety	Wason	1922	Brill 77E1	4-GE258	K-35	

EQUIPMENT NOTES

1. All old equipment of Bangor Street Railway disposed of by 1907.
2. No. 30 sold to Fairfield & Shawmut Street Railway.
3. No. 68 rebuilt into service car.
4. Semi-convertible cars Nos. 80 through 96 converted for one-man operation.
5. No. 42 Birney was ex-Concord, Maynard & Hudson Street Railway (Mass.) No. 200, acquired through an equipment broker in 1923; scrapped 1926 after wreck.
6. Three single truck center entrance cars sold to an equipment broker in 1920.
7. Two 35-ft. closed cars with smoking compartments known to have been on the road but no details are available. Originally used on Penobscot Central; sold to Waterville, Fairfield & Oakland Railway.
8. Under Bangor Hydro-Electric managment the rolling stock consisted of the double truck safety cars 6-18 (even numbers) all sold to Johnstown Traction Co. (Penna.) in 1942; Birneys 20-66 (even numbers) and semi-convertibles 80-96 (even numbers).
9. At time of road's closing, December 31, 1945, passenger rolling stock consisted of 14 Birney cars available for operation.
10. Absence of car numbers for closed cars in the 50 series is due to fact that these had been ex-Bangor, Orono & Old Town 4-wheel cars disposed of at an early date. Most bodies were acquired by company officials and hauled to lake and river sites for use as cottages.

END OF THE LINE— Bangor Hydro-Electric Co. Birney No. 22 is shown here both pictorially and time-wise at the "end of the line." The date was April 22, 1946, almost four months after the cars ceased running in Bangor when Harold L. Goldsmith took this picture. The cars had been placed on temporary rail outside the carhouse to await possible resale. Shortly after that same spring they were sold for scrap metal and cut up.

BANGOR RAILWAY & ELECTRIC COMPANY
CAR ROSTER 1905 - 1924

OPEN CARS

Car No.	Type of Car	Builder	Year Built	Trucks	Motors	Control	Notes
1	10-bench	Brill	1907	Brill 21E	2-GE80	K-10	
3	10-bench	Brill	1907	Brill 21E	2-GE80	K-10	
5	10-bench	Brill	1907	Brill 21E	2-GE80	K-10	
7	10-bench	Brill	1907	Brill 21E	2-GE80	K-10	
9	13-bench	Laconia	1912	Baldwin	2-WH306	K-36G	Vestibule front
11	13-bench	Laconia	1912	Baldwin	2-WH306	K-36G	Vestibule front
13	13-bench	Laconia	1912	Baldwin	2-WH306	K-36G	Vestibule front
15	15-bench	Laconia (?)					Ex-Penobscot Central. No info.
17	15-bench	Laconia (?)					Ex-Penobscot Central. No info.
53	10-bench	Briggs	1895	Brill 22E	2-GE80	K-10	Ex-Bangor, Orono & Old Town
55	10-bench	Briggs	1895	Brill 22E	2-GE80	K-10	Ex-Bangor, Orono & Old Town
57	10-bench	Briggs	1895	Brill 22E	2-GE80	K-10	Ex-Bangor, Orono & Old Town
59	10-bench	Briggs	1895	Brill 22E	2-GE80	K-10	Ex-Bangor, Orono & Old Town
61	10-bench	Briggs	1895	Brill 22E	2-GE80	K-10	Ex-Bangor, Orono & Old Town
63	10-bench	Briggs	1895	Brill 22E	2-GE80	K-10	Ex-Bangor, Orono & Old Town
65	10-bench	Briggs	1895	Brill 22E	2-GE80	K-10	Ex-Bangor, Orono & Old Town
101	10-bench	Brill	1897	Brill 22E	2-GE80	K-10	Ex-Bangor, Hampden & W'np't
103	10-bench	Brill	1897	Brill 22E	2-GE80	K-10	Ex-Bangor, Hampden & W'np't
105	10-bench	Brill	1897	Brill 22E	2-GE80	K-10	Ex-Bangor, Hampden & W'np't
107	10-bench	Jacks'n & Sharpe	1897				Possibly ex-Penobscot Central

WORK & SERVICE CARS

Car No.		Builder	Year Built	Trucks	Motors	Control	Notes
M-1	Shear plow	Wason	1903	Wason	2-GE67	K-10	Ex-Eastern Mass. P-366
M-2	Shear plow	Wason	1904	Wason	2-GE67	K-10	
M-3	Nose plow	Pollard & Grothe			2-GE67	K-10	
M-4	Nose plow				2-GE67	K-10	
M-5	Shear plow	Wason		Wason	2-WH306	K-36G	
M-6	Rotary plow	Ruggles	1901	Peckham			
M-7	Line car	Bangor Ry & El	1916	Brill 21E	2-GE800	K-4	
M-8	Sprinkler			Brill 21E	2-GE800	K	
M-9	Gravel car			Brill 21E	2-GE70	K-10	
M-10	Nose plow	Wason		Wason	2-GE80	K-11	
M-11	Gravel car			Brill 21E	2-GE67	K-10	
M-12	Dump car	Magor	1912	Arch bar	4-GE80	K-28B	
M-13	Track grinder	Kerwin	1912				
M-14	Electric shovel	Bangor Ry & El	1912	Brill 27G	2-GE80	K-10	
M-15							
M-16	Derrick			Arch bar			
M-17	Sand car	Newburyport		Brill 21E	2-GE800	K	
M-18	Sand car	Brill		Brill 21E	2-WH306	K-36	
M-19							
M-20	Motor flat	Bangor Ry & El		Baldwin	4-GE80	K-28	
M-21	Flat car						
M-22	Dump car						
S-68	Service car	Brill	1902	Brill 27G			Former passenger car
	Rotary substat'n						Former box express trailer

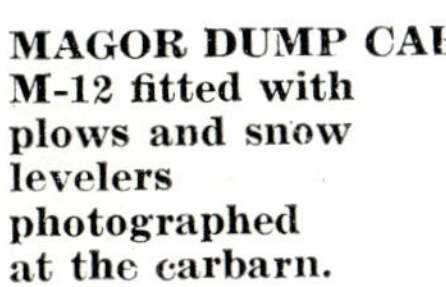

MAGOR DUMP CAR M-12 fitted with plows and snow levelers photographed at the carbarn.

BANGOR RAILWAY & ELECTRIC COMPANY
FREIGHT & EXPRESS CARS

Car No.	Type	Builder	Year Built	Trucks	Motors	Control	Notes
2	32-ft. box trailer	ACF	1915	Arch bar			
4	32-ft. box trailer	ACF	1915	Arch bar			
6	32-ft. box trailer	ACF	1915	Arch bar			
8	28-ft. box trailer	Portland Co.	1898				Ex-Penobscot Central
10	28-ft. box trailer	Portland Co.	1898				Ex-Penobscot Central
12	28-ft. box trailer	Portland Co.	1898				Ex-Penobscot Central
14	28-ft. box trailer	Portland Co.	1898				Ex-Penobscot Central
16	28-ft. box trailer	Portland Co.	1898				Ex-Penobscot Central
18	28-ft. 6-in. box tr.	Portland Co.	1898				Ex-Penobscot Central
20	28-ft. 6-in. box tr.	Portland Co.	1898				Ex-Penobscot Central
1	32-ft. flat trailer	ACF	1915	Arch bar			
3	32-ft. flat trailer	ACF	1915	Arch bar			
5	32-ft. flat trailer	ACF	1915	Arch bar			
7	30-ft. flat trailer	Portland Co.	1898				Ex-Penobscot Central
9	30-ft. flat trailer	Portland Co.	1898				Ex-Penobscot Central
11	30-ft. flat trailer	Portland Co.	1898				Ex-Penobscot Central
13	30-ft. flat trailer	Portland Co.	1898				Ex-Penobscot Central
15	30-ft. flat trailer	Portland Co.	1898				Ex-Penobscot Central
102	Box express	Brill	1910	Brill 27MCB	4-GE80	K-28	
104	Box express			Arch bar	4-GE80	K-28	
106	Box express	Wason	1913	Brill 27MCB	4-GE80	K-28	
108	Box express	Brill	1897		4-GE80		Ex-BH&W No. 7 (4-wheel)
108	Box express	Laconia		Brill 27MCB	4-GE80	K-35G2	Ex-Brockton & Plymouth St. Ry.

NOTE
The original gasoline-electric car of the Penobscot Central was rebuilt to an express
motor but is not shown on any available roster.

EXPRESS MOTOR No. 108 (second 108) as it looked in the 1930s. This Laconia-built car came from Brockton & Plymouth
Street Railway in wartime 1918 and went to the Springfield (Vt.) Terminal Railway, along with No. 106, in wartime 1942.

BANGOR STREET RAILWAY
Rolling Stock Report

Year	Closed	Open	Plows	Work	Trailer	Other
1889	5	4	1	0	0	0
1890	15	15	1	0	0	0
1891	15	15	1	0	0	0
1892	15	15	1	0	0	0
1893	10	15	2	0	0	0
1894	11	15	2	0	0	0
1895	11	17	2	1	0	1
1896	11	15	2	0	2	1
1897	10	14	2	1	5*	0
1898	10	14	2	1	4	0
1899	13	15	2	1	0	0
1900	13	15	2	1	0	0
1901	11	13	2	0	0	0
1902	11	13	2	0	0	0
1903	11	13	2	0	0	0
1904	14	17	3	0	0	0
1905	14	17	3	0	0	0

*4 box passengers trailers.

NOTE:　Annual reports from 1901 through 1904 listed 2 electric automobiles, purchased to transport passengers across Penobscot River toll bridge for those transferring to the Brewer Division. The bridge was washed out in the 1902 freshet. These early electric automobiles are one of the first attempts at regular motor bus operation jointly with street railway service.

Other Bangor Street Railway cars were purchased second hand for use as trailers and later motorized, but official annual reports do not list them separately.

BANGOR, ORONO & OLD TOWN RY.
Rolling Stock Report

Year	Closed	Open	Freight Motor	Freight Trailer	Work Cars	Plows	Other
1895	6	8	0	0	1	2	0
1896	6	8	0	0	1	2	0
1897	8	8	1*	0	1	2	0
1898	8	8	1	0	1	2	0
1899	8	8	1	0	1	2	0
1900	8	8	0	0	1	2	0
1901	8	8	0	0	1	2	0
1902	8	8	0	0	1	2	0
1903	7	8	0	0	1	2	0
1904	8	2	0	0	1	2	0
1905	8	2	0	0	1	2	0

*West End Street Railway (Boston)

SERVICE CARS AND PLOWS of Bangor Hydro-Electric Co. are shown in these pictures taken at the carbarn circa 1930. M-8 was the street sprinkler, M-5 with M-10 behind it were Wason 4-wheel plows while M-20 doubled as a work car and a snow plow with wings for leveling the snow after it was piled alongside the tracks in the main city streets.

BANGOR, HAMPDEN & WINTERPORT RAILWAY

Rolling Stock Report

Year	Closed	Open	Freight Motor	Freight Trailer	Work Cars	Plows	Other
1897	4*	4	0	0	1	1	0
1898	4	4	0	0	1	1	0
1899	4	6	0	0	2	1	0
1900	4	6	0	0	2	1	0
1901	4	6	0	0	2	1	0
1902	4	6	0	0	2	1	0
1903	4	6	0	0	2	1	0
1904	4	6	0	0	2	1	0
1905	4	6	0	0	2	1	0

*One combination type.

PENOBSCOT CENTRAL RAILWAY
Rolling Stock Report

Year	Closed	Open	Freight Motor	Freight Trailer	Work Cars	Plows	Other
1899	2*	0	0	20	0	1	0
1900	No report. Road dormant, being electrified.						
1901	3	2	2	20	0	1	0
1902	5	2	2	20	0	2	0
1903	6**	2§	2	20	0	2	0
1904	6**	2§	2	20	0	2	0
1905	6**	5§	2	20	0	2	0
1906	6**	5§	2	20	1	2	0

*Includes 1 closed passenger trailer.
§Includes 2 open bench trailers in 1903 & 1904; 4 open bench trailers in 1905 & 1906.
**Includes 1 closed passenger trailer in 1903 & 1904; 2 closed passenger trailers 1905 & 1906.

NOTE: Laconia Car Co. order book lists following:
1898—Order No. 85. 1 Motor Car for Penobscot Central (Patten Gas-Electric Body).
1898—Order No. 87. 1 Combination Car for Penobscot Central. (No other details available).

COLD WEATHER SECRET — These patented storm windows that were installed on cars like No. 92 for the winter season, along with electric heaters, kept the trolleys on the Old Town line toasty and warm on Maine's coldest days.

NO. 92 SEMI-CONVERTIBLE is shown in this Wason builder's photo taken in 1914. Similar cars were built for other roads.

Bangor Railway & Electric Co.   Bangor Hydro-Electric Co.
Cars on the Roster, 1905-1945

Year	Closed	Open	Freight Motor	Freight Trailer	Work Cars	Plows	Other	Sprinkler	Notes
1905	25	24	0	0	3	6	1	0	
1906	29	25	3	20*	3	7	1	0	*10 box, 10 flat
1907	24	22	3	20	2	6	1	0	
1908	25	23	3	20	2	6	0	0	
1909	25	23	3	20	2	6	0	0	
1910	26	24	2	20	2	6	0	1	
1911	28	24	2	20	2	6	0	1	
1912	26	22	3	20	3	6	0	1	
1913	26	22	3	20	4	7	0	1	
1914	31	22	3	20	3	7	0	1	
1915	31	22	3	19*	3	7	1	1	*1 box to Rotary Sub-Station
1916	31	22	3	18	3	7	5	1	
1917	36*	20	3	18	3	7	5	1	*1 Center Ent. Tr.
1918	39*	20	4	18	3	7	5	1	*1 Center Ent. Tr.
1919	51	20	4	18	3	7	6	1	
1920	39	10	4	23	6	6	1	1	
1921	39	8	4	16	8	6	2	1	
1922	45	3	4	12	9	5	1*	1	*Rail grinder
1923	44	0	4	12	9	6	1	1	
1924	35*	0	4	12	10	6	1	1	*All one-man cars
1925	35	0	4	12	10	6	1	1	
1926	33	0	4	12	9	6	1	1	
1927	33	0	4	12	8	7	1	1	
1928	33	0	4	12	8	7	1	1	
1929	33	0	4	12	8	7	1	1	
1930	33	0	4	12	6	7	1	1	
1931	33	0	3	12	4	6	1	1	
1932	33	0	3	12	4	6	1	1	
1933	33	0	3	12	3	6	1	1	
1934	33	0	3	12	3	6	1	1	
1935	33	0	3	12	3	6	1	1	
1936	33	0	3	12	2	7	1	0	
1937	33	0	3	7	2	7	1	0	
1938	33	0	3	1	0	7	1	0	
1939	31	0	2	1	2	6	1	0	
1940	29	0	2	1	1	5	1	0	
1941	16	0	1	1	0	4	1	0	
1942	16	0	1	1	0	4	1	0	
1943	16	0	1	0	0	2	1	0	
1944	16	0	1	0	0	2	1	0	
1945	16	0	1	0	0	2	1	0	

A Motorman Who Was A Radio 'Ham'

THE LATE Guy Webster, old-time motorman on the Bangor system, and one who assisted this writer with information for this history, was—in his younger days—a radio "ham."

He wired a radio key into the buzzer system of his regular car. While out on the line, he would occasionally flash a "CQ, CQ, CQ" over the buzzer system of the car. This in radio parlance is a signal inviting anyone listening in to respond.

Guy related that from time to time he would receive a message in return from some car rider who was "hep" to the radio jargon, using the button on the post near the passenger's seat.

In this manner he became acquainted with a goodly number of radio "hams" in the Bangor area.

WORK TRAIN unloads new poles along State Street with a three-man crew using one pole braced against the flat car and a series of cables to lift each pole off the flat car and lower it to the street where it was rolled to the curb for setting another day.

BANGOR STREET RAILWAY

Financial Record

Year	Passengers	Passenger Revenue	Total Revenue	Operating Expense	Taxes & Interest	Profit & Loss	Surplus or Deficit
1889	215,546	$11,324	$11,434	$ 5,337	$ 700	$ 5,356	(5 months)
1890	616,258	34,071	34,071	20,239	5,200	8,632	$16,667
1891	817,457	43,457	42,812	29,499	11,627	1,686	
1892	No record	44,890	45,038	33,258	11,670	109	1,795
1893	892,212	47,213	47,567	38,229	11,580	2,353—	558—
1894	1,017,000	50,850	50,928	50,006	12,263	12,331—	12,889—
1895	1,132,006	56,600	56,790	46,280	13,086	2,544—	14,875—
1896	1,293,861	52,071	58,071	51,354	12,000	5,283—	7,827—
1897	1,560,771	64,291	69,493	59,044	12,000	1,551—	9,378—
1898	1,523,837	61,933	65,291	54,161	12,788	1,660—	11,038—
1899	1,522,966	61,664	63,674	49,099	12,881	1,694	9,343—
1900	1,563,418	63,418	65,171	50,548	10,841	3,782	5,561—
1901	1,309,518	65,494	67,155	51,331	10,958	4,866	694—
1902	1,208,216	60,432	65,888	63,174	11,101	8,387—	9,081—
1903	1,404,694	70,316	74,876	55,418	11,791	7,667	1,414—
1904	1,656,293	82,852	86,791	54,707	11,562	20,522	985
1905	1,309,908	65,908	69,231	44,550	8,838	15,843	14,429

(Fiscal year 1905 through March 31.)

BANGOR, ORONO & OLD TOWN RAILWAY

Financial Record

Year	Passengers	Passenger Revenue	Total Revenue	Operating Expense	Taxes & Interest	Profit & Loss	Surplus or Deficit
1896	1,060,314	$55,766	$56,122	$29,466	$ 7,650	$19,006	$ 3,000 Div.
1897	1,268,642	64,474	65,659	41,637	17,476	6,546	12,000 Div.
1898	1,225,028	61,251	63,676	56,231	9,736	2,290—	8,000 Div.
1899	943,927	47,196	49,182	35,668	13,381	133	
1900	984,700	49,235	50,087	36,674	8,723	5,190	
1901	1,028,874	52,594	53,656	38,073	9,930	5,653	
1902	1,152,848	57,230	57,680	65,224	10,309	17,853—	
1903	1,213,513	58,630	60,850	48,854	12,381	385	
1904	1,130,301	59,162	61,162	41,476	13,242	7,190	
1905	960,564	47,215	49,089	34,471	10,570	4,047	To 3-31-05.

BANGOR, HAMPDEN & WINTERPORT RAILWAY

Financial Record

Year	Passengers	Passenger Revenue	Total Revenue	Operating Expense	Taxes & Interest	Profit & Loss—
1898	161,186	8,569	9,081	8,582	596	96—
1899	397,560	20,609	22,584	19,535	2,278	771
1900	464,722	24,086	26,817	22,986	2,624	1,207
1901	397,336	21,906	24,703	15,460	8,676	566
1902	435,721	23,848	26,681	22,640	2,718	1,324
1903	512,144	26,345	27,484	16,701	9,485	2,431
1904	503,923	25,201	27,357	15,773	7,936	3,649
1905	431,013	21,352	23,388	13,356	6,635	3,397 To 3-31-05.

PENOBSCOT CENTRAL — BANGOR & NORTHERN

Financial Record

Year	Passengers	Passenger Revenue	Freight Revenue	Total Revenue	Operating Expense	Taxes & Interest	Profit & Loss—	Surplus or Deficit—
1899	$	$ 102	$ 356	$ 146	$	$	$ 146	$ 146
1900	No report filed; road was being rebuilt for conventional trolley operation.							
1901	12,216	2,959	1,309	4,268	2,269	60	1,939—	105,136—
1902	195,548	14,477	14,170	29,742	18,108	6,416	5,218	99,518—
1903	368,464	18,423	14,411	38,807	32,777	12,692	11,662—	111,429—
1904	311,801	15,590	16,328	33,007	32,227	12,500	11,369—	122,798—
1905	276,965	13,848	15,242	30,016	42,040	12,797	24,821—	147,562—
1905	35,323	1,766	631	2,486	1,409	28	1,262	146,299—
1906	45,189	1,091		2,071	14,602	2,143	3,369	

NOTE: Penobscot Central to 7-28-1905; Bangor & Northern through 1-31-1906.
—Minus sign indicates loss or deficit.

Bangor Railway & Electric Co.

Year	Net Earnings from Railway Operations	Fare Passengers Carried
1905	$ 95,000	999,834
(March 31 to June 30)		
1906	95,000	4,414,715
1907	103,283	4,607,694
1908	107,609	4,857,840
1909	108,818	4,956,103
1910	118,126	5,242,648
1911	118,162	5,287,916
1912	139,906	5,740,245
1913	128,855	6,008,902
1914	166,135	6,522,962
1915	161,918	6,571,038
1916	122,874	6,403,924
1917	80,964	7,001,884
1918	33,125	7,604,862
1919	117,647	7,272,588
1920	103,921	7,683,659
1921	151,168	7,835,046
1922	104,730	7,469,733
1923	86,920	7,005,652
1924	49,594	6,171,753
1925	23,576	932,929
(First 3 months 1925)		

Bangor Hydro-Electric Co.

Year	Net Earnings from Railway Operations	Fare Passengers Carried
1925	88,156	3,430,235
(9 months of 1925)		
1926	128,304	4,347,481
1927	92,180	3,861,682
1928	96,370	3,593,894
1929	68,195	3,333,340
1930	64,570	3,157,561
1931	31,921	2,561,286
1932	21,413—	2,167,937
1933	9,480	2,764,740
1934	729	3,016,439
1935	7,220—	2,978,408
1936	8,502—	2,939,820
1937	15,428—	2,879,114
1938	19,675—	2,814,895
1939	16,894—	2,788,945
1940	61,149—	2,860,813
1941	120,227—	1,751,857
1942	4,811	1,314,443
(To September 30th)		

Penobscot Transportation Co.

Year	Net Earnings from Railway Operations	Fare Passengers Carried
1942	10,453	544,240
(October 1 - December 31)		
1943	47,615	2,749,554
1944	37,188	2,882,948
1945	31,609	3,022,676

Book of Rules for Bangor's Trolleymen

THE BOOK of Rules and Regulations for the guidance of motormen and conductors of Bangor's street railway system is reproduced on the following pages:

RULE BOOK NO.

This Book is the Property of the

**BANGOR RAILWAY &
ELECTRIC COMPANY**

and is issued to

Name ....
Position ....
Division ....
Date ....

Who hereby agrees to return it to the proper officer of the Company when called for, or upon leaving the service.

NOTICE

Conductors and motormen are expected to have a copy of these Rules and Regulations with them at all times, and to make frequent study of same.

Wilful or careless violation of the Rules and Regulations (either in this book or the Special Orders at the stations) will be deemed sufficient cause for dismissal.

Ignorance of any of the Rules or Orders will not be accepted as an excuse for non-compliance with the same.

This book must be returned in good condition to the Superintendent of Railway before any settlement will be made with any employee leaving the service of the Company.

INTRODUCTION

The employee, while on duty, is the representative of the Company to the public. Whatever the Company is forbidden to do, he must not do. Whatever the Company is required to do, he must do, so far as his duties are applicable.

The success and reputation of the Company, to a large extent, depend upon his civility, his honesty, his good judgment, his tact, and his ability to get along with all persons.

While the road is intended and expected to be a source of profit to the Company, at the same time, it must serve the public. It was built for the convenience of the people, and there should be an earnest effort on the part of each employee to make the service so excellent that the public will find the road worthy of patronage. In this way, the interest of the Company can best be secured.

It is expected that the employees will obey to the letter the instructions given in stated cases, but cases will arise in which no instructions have been given. When these occur it is expected that the employees will use good, sound judgment.

Employees are expected to read the following instructions carefully and often, until they know just what to do in every case without referring to this book, and will be required to pass an examination in regard to their knowledge of the same when called upon.

All Employees whose duties are prescribed by these rules will be furnished with a copy, for which they will sign a receipt, and will be required to have the same in their possession at all times while on duty.

GENERAL RULES

1. **When Brakes Are Out of Order—** You are hereby notified that you must never attempt to operate your car when you know that the brakes are not in working order. You must remain wherever you are at the time you discover your brakes are disabled and telephone the Inspector. The conductor will be held equally responsible for failure to comply with this rule.

2. **Knowledge of Rules—**Conductors and motormen are required to be familiar with the rules, and with every special order issued. The bulletin board must be examined daily for special orders. Employment by the company binds the employee to comply with the rules and regulations, and ignorance

SNOW AND ICE packed in the flangeways had sent No. 54 off the rails on the State Street bridge in this wartime 1940s view.

BOOK OF RULES—Continued

thereof will not be accepted as an excuse for negligence or omission of duty. If in doubt as to the exact meaning of any rule or special order, application must be made to the proper authority for information and instruction.

3. Report for Duty — Regular conductors and motormen must report for duty five minutes before leaving time for their first trip, or, if for any good reason unable to so report, must give notice at least one hour before such leaving time.

Extra men must report at such time as ordered, or must give notice at least one hour before such time. They must not absent themselves after answering roll call without permission.

4. Personal Appearance — Conductors and motormen must report for duty clothed in full regulation uniform, and must be clean and neat in appearance.

5. Politeness—Conductors and motormen must treat all passengers with politeness; avoid difficulty and exercise patience, forbearance and self-control under all conditions. They must not make threatening gestures, or use loud, uncivil, indecent or profane language, even under the greatest provocation.

6. Habits and Personal Conduct— The following acts are prohibited:

(a) Drinking intoxicating liquors of any kind while on duty.

(b) Entering any place where the same is sold as a beverage while in uniform or while on duty, except in a case of necessity.

(c) Constant frequenting of drinking places.

(d) Carrying any intoxicating drink about the person while on duty.

(e) Carrying intoxicating drinks on the company's premises at any time.

(f) Indulging to excess in intoxicating liquors at any time.

(g) Gambling in any form, including the laying of bets (and playing raffles) while upon the premises of the company.

(h) Smoking tobacco while on duty.

(i) Smoking tobacco while off duty in any part of the company's building.

7. Talking to Motormen—Motormen while operating cars are permitted to answer questions of superior officers and to give proper instructions to students only. All other conversation with motormen while car is in motion is forbidden.

8. Run on Time—Cars must never be run ahead of schedule time, but must pass time points and leave terminals promptly on time, unless unavoidably delayed.

9. Railroad Crossings—Cars must be brought to a full stop, at a safe distance, approaching steam railroad crossings at grade, and motormen must not proceed until conductor has gone ahead to the center of the crossing, looking both ways, and given the "Come ahead" sig-

nal. Before starting, the motorman will look back to see that no passengers are getting on or off; and in no case proceed even after the conductor's signal, until he has also examined the crossing and satisfied himself that steam cars are not approaching.

When there is more than one track the conductor must remain in advance of the car until the last track is reached.

Where crossing is protected by derail, interlocking plant or flagman (employed by the company) this rule does not apply, special instructions being issued to govern.

10. Starting Cars After Blockades— In the event of a blockade of cars from any cause, all cars in such blockade must not be started at one time, but only singly and at such intervals as will not burden the feeder line.

11. Reporting Defects — Conductors and motormen will report to foreman or inspector any defect in car, track or wire which needs immediate attention.

12. Hearing by Superintendent — A hearing will be given by the superintendent to every employee who desires to complain. Reports or suggestions for the betterment of the service will always receive consideration.

RULES FOR CONDUCTORS

13. Be on Rear Platform—Remain on rear platform when not collecting fares, keeping a lookout for persons desiring to board car.

Keep careful watch of passengers to observe requests to stop car.

When stops are made at principal streets, places of amusement, churches, or at any point where a considerable number of passengers enter or leave the car, conductors must be on rear platform until such point is passed.

14. Announcements—Announce distinctly the names of streets, public places and transfer points when approaching the same.

15. Removing Trolley — Do not remove trolley from wire at end of run, or elsewhere at night, until passengers have alighted from car.

16. Route Signs — See that route signs are properly displayed on each trip.

17. Carrying Packages—Passengers must not be allowed to carry bulky or dangerous packages aboard cars.

18. Lost Articles—An employee finding a lost article in the cars, waiting-rooms or on the property of this Company will forward same to the proper officer.

Do not in any way take possession of, or assume responsibility for, any package which a passenger may bring upon the car, excepting such articles as are to be turned into the Lost Article Department.

19. Watching the Trolley — Keep your hand upon the trolley rope when passing over switches, crossings, or going around curves. Should the trolley leave the wire, the conductor must at once pull down the trolley and signal the motorman to stop. After the car has stopped replace the trolley on the wire, look around and through the car and see if any persons are boarding or leaving same; ring two bells for the motorman to start. See that passengers keep their hands off the trolley rope.

20. Housing Cars—When the car is run in the house, either day or night, remove trolley from the wire (if equipped with overhead trolley) and turn to position ready for leaving.

21. Moving Forward — On closed cars, when standing passengers crowd the rear door, request them to "Please step forward in the car."

22. Seating Passengers — Standing passengers should be directed to vacant seats, and an effort made to provide them with seats where possible.

23. Assisting Passengers — Elderly and feeble persons, and women and children, should be given assistance getting on and off car, when possible.

24. Dogs in Cars—No dogs should be allowed on a car except such small dogs as can be carried in the laps of passengers.

RULES FOR MOTORMEN

25. Stopping for Passengers—Keep a careful lookout on both sides of the street and bring the car to a full stop for every person who signals, except that when a car has considerable headway, is overcrowded, and another car follows within the same block (or 200 feet), passengers should be requested to take the following car.

Cars will stop on signal only at marked crossings, at car stations, transfer points and at points as provided in special orders.

26. Churches and Hospitals—When passing a church during the hours of service, and at all times when passing a hospital, do not use the current and do not ring the gong, unless necessary.

27. Reversing Car — Never use the reversing lever to stop car except to avoid a collision or injuring a person or animal, or when the brake rigging is disabled.

Do not reverse the power when the brake is set, but release the brake and reverse the power simultaneously, and, when the reverse lever is thrown in position, apply the current one point at a time, otherwise the fuse will melt or the breaker will release. Sand should be used when making an emergency stop.

28. Passing Cars—Never run against the switch point of crossover when meeting a car, but slacken speed sufficiently to allow the car moving in the opposite direction to pass before striking switch point.

This rule refers particularly to all crossovers having switch points facing opposite to the direction in which the car is moving.

29. Leaving Car—Never leave platform of car without taking controller handle, throwing off the overhead switch and applying the brake. Be careful to see that the hands point to the "off" mark before taking off controller handle.

30. Economical Use of Current—In order to effect an economical use of electric current, it is necessary that the continuous movements of starting and increasing speed should be made gradually.

In starting a car, let it run until the maximum speed of each notch has been obtained before moving handle to the next notch.

Do not apply brakes when the current is on. Do not apply current when brakes are applied.

Do not allow the current to remain on when car is going down grade, or when passing over section breakers. Endeavor to run car with the least amount of current, allowing the car to drift without the use of the current when it can be done without falling behind time.

A great amount of power can be saved by using judgment and discretion in approaching stopping places and switches by shutting off the power so as to allow the car to drift to the stopping places or switch without a too vigorous use of the brake.

31. Throwing Overhead Switch—An overhead switch must never be thrown until power is turned entirely off, except in case controller cylinder fails to turn when power is on. It must be thrown by hand only.

32. Power Off Line—When the power leaves the line the controller must be shut off, and the overhead switch thrown, the light switch turned on, and the car started only when the lamps burn brightly.

33. Release Brakes Before Stop—When brakes are set to make a stop they should always be released, or nearly so, just before the car comes to a standstill.

34. Water on Track—When there is water on the track, run the car very slowly, drifting without use of power whenever possible, otherwise there is danger of burning out the motors.

35. Sanded Rails—Never run on freshly sanded rails with brakes full on, except to prevent an accident, as the wheels are liable to be flattened when this is done. On cars provided with sand boxes, in case of slippery rail, always sand the track for a short distance before applying the brakes.

36. "Spinning" of Wheels—Care must be taken, particularly during snowstorms, to avoid "spinning" of the wheels with no forward or backward movement of the car.

37. Do Not Slide Wheels—On a slippery rail do not allow wheels to slide; as soon as wheels commence to slide the brake must be released and reset.

38. Do Not Oil Car—Do not oil or grease any part of a car.

SIGNALS AND THEIR APPLICATION

The following code of bell signals will be used in the operation of the car:

39. Bell Signals—From conductor to motorman, to be given on motorman's signal bell:

One Bell—"Stop at next crossing or station."

Two Bells—"Go ahead."

NO. 20 on Main St., Bangor, going to Hampden on new Bangor, Hampden & Winterport Railway before arrival of their cars.

BOOK OF RULES—Continued

Two Bells — When car is moving "Stop immediately."

Three Bells — Given when car is standing—"Back car slowly."

From motorman to conductor, given on conductor's bell.

One Bell—"Come ahead."

Two Bells—"Watch the trolley and danger signal to the conductor."

Three Bells—Signal to conductor that motorman desires to back car.

Four Bells—"Set rear brake."

Whenever a car in service is stopped, the motorman will, as soon as he is ready to go forward, give two taps of the gong, after which, if the conductor is ready to proceed, he will give the regular "go ahead" signal—two bells.

The motorman will answer the signal to stop from the conductor by one loud tap of gong and two loud taps of gong after receiving the signal to go ahead. If unable to proceed immediately upon receipt of signal, motorman will wait for another "go ahead" signal before starting the car.

When the car is standing and motorman desires to back, for any reason, he will give the conductor three bells, but must not move the car until he has changed the handles to the rear end. If the distance is more than ten feet, the conductor will change the trolley.

40. Danger Signals — Red lights or flags indicate danger, and when they are placed alongside the track, cars must be run slowly and with caution. When placed on the track, cars must come to a full stop until such signal is removed.

41. Signals Before Passing Obstructions Near Track—Before passing any vehicle or obstruction close to the track, where passengers or conductor are liable to be injured while standing on the step of an open car, motorman must give two taps of signal bell as warning, reduce speed, and assure himself that all is clear before proceeding.

42. Starting—Motorman must never move car (whether stopped on signal or for any other reason) without signal from conductor, and then only when assured that no one is getting on or off front platform.

Conductor must never give signal to start when passengers are getting on or off.

PRECAUTIONARY RULES—
ACCIDENTS

43. Safety — The safety of passengers is the first consideration. All employees are required to exercise constant care to prevent injury to persons or property, and in all cases of doubt take the safe side.

44. Persons Between Cars — Cars moving in opposite directions must not pass at points where persons are standing between the tracks, but must be operated so as not to occupy both tracks at such points simultaneously.

45. Patrols—When any police or fire department vehicle is observed approaching (from any direction) cars must be stopped until such vehicle has passed.

46. Ambulances—Ambulances must be allowed the right of way, and when approaching or passing, cars must be kept under control to avoid collision.

47. Warning to Passengers — Conductors and motormen must (in a polite way) endeavor to keep people from jumping on and off the cars while in motion.

If such people attempt to get on or off the car while it is in motion, notify them politely to wait until the car stops. If passengers are leaving car while another car is approaching from the opposite direction notify them politely to look out for car on other track.

48. Standing on Steps—Do not allow anyone to stand on the steps or buffers, and never, under any circumstances, permit a woman or child to ride on the steps. They should be fully inside of the car before signal is given to start.

49. Leaving Car — When necessary for conductor to leave his car he must notify the motorman to protect passengers and car. Should passengers board car during absence of conductor, motorman will notify conductor of the number and location of such passengers upon his return.

Cars in commission must not be left unprotected, either conductor or motorman always remaining in charge.

50. Exercise Care — Motormen are cautioned to exercise great care when a vehicle is passing alongside of track ahead of car. Ring the gong vigorously to attract the attention of the person driving as a warning not to pull in ahead of car, and run cautiously until the vehicle is passed in safety.

Gong must also be rung at all street intersections.

51. Passing Cars — When passing standing cars gong must be rung and car brought to slow speed.

52. Render Assistance—In case of accident, however slight, to persons or property in connection with or near any car, the motorman and conductor in charge of the same will render all assistance necessary and practicable. In no case will they leave injured persons without first having seen that they are cared for.

53. Medical Attendance—Motormen or conductors are directed not to employ medical attendance to injured persons, except for the first visit, in cases of personal injury; nor will they visit such persons at any other time afterward, unless specially instructed so to do by an officer of the company.

54. Fatal Accidents—In the event of a fatal accident it will not be necessary to blockade the line awaiting the arrival of the coroner or any other official. If any accident occurs where it is impossible to carry the body to a place of shelter and security, motorman and conductor will put the body on the car and convey it to some suitable place.

55. Reports to Be Full and Complete—A full and complete report of every accident, no matter how trivial, and whether occurring on or near the car, must be made by the conductor. Accidents sometimes considered as not worth reporting are often the most serious, troublesome and expensive.

The conductor will obtain the name and residence in full of all witnesses on or near the car.

The motorman will assist the conductor in securing the names of witnesses whenever practicable, and he will be held responsible for any neglect to render assistance.

In all cases full facts must be obtained and stated in the report as follows:

The date, exact time, exact place, run and car number, and the direction in which the car was moving, the nature of the accident or collision, and the cause of its occurrence.

The full name and address of the party injured or whose vehicle was in collision (giving the names of both the driver and the owner of the vehicle.)

Ascertain the extent of injuries or damage, if any, before leaving the spot.

In case there has been an accident on the car, and the conductors change ahead, the conductor taking car on which the accident happened must secure the names of witnesses as above.

In case a person is struck by a car after passing around the rear of a standing car, the numbers of both cars must be obtained, and both crews shall report accident.

If any accident is caused by any defect or damaged condition of car, conductor must report the same and its cause.

Accidents to employees will be reported the same as accidents to passengers.

Any trouble or disturbance of a boisterous or quarrelsome character which occurs on a car, or the ejectment of a person from a car, will be reported as an accident.

56. Telephone Information—In case of accident involving personal injury or serious damage to property, conductor will telephone at once to headquarters, giving notice and particulars of accident.

In case of a blockade, where assistance is required to get cars moving, conductor of car in block must perform this duty. Expense of telephone message will be refunded upon application at office.

57. Report of Accidents to Inspectors—Conductors and motormen will make a verbal report to the first inspector or official they meet of any accident, blockade or mishap of any kind.

58. Give Information to Proper Persons—No employee shall under any circumstances, give any information whatever concerning any accident, delay, blockade or mishap of any kind to any person except to a properly authorized representative of the company.

59. Responsibility for Damages—Employees will be held answerable for any damages caused by their neglect or carelessness or by disobedience of rules.

60. Disabled Cars—The motorman or conductor of any disabled car, withdrawn from the track, must remain with the car until relieved by proper authority or until car reaches depot.

EJECTMENTS

61. Ejectments—No passenger shall be forcibly ejected from a car from any cause whatsoever without order of an inspector, starter or official of the company, unless the conduct of the passenger is dangerous or grossly offensive. In such case the ejectment must be made by the conductor with the assistance of the motorman after the car has been brought to a stop, using "only such force as is sufficient to expel the offending passenger with a reasonable regard for his personal safety."

62. Refusing to Pay Fares—Transfers—When a passenger refuses to pay fare or presents a defective transfer, or ticket, upon which, in the judgment of the conductor, the passenger is not entitled to ride, the conductor must secure the names of as many witnesses to the fact as is possible, whereupon the car must be stopped and the passenger requested to leave. If the passenger fails to comply with such request, the facts of the case must be brought to the attention of the first inspector, starter or official. In all cases the passenger must be given the benefit of any doubt.

When a passenger who refuses to pay fare requests to be allowed to leave the car, the car must be stopped and the person permitted to alight.

63. Intoxication—No passenger will be ejected from a car for mere intoxication, unless said passenger becomes dangerous or offensive; such passenger must be then ejected with great care and must be guided until free from probable injury.

64. Spitting on Floor—No passenger will be ejected from a car for spitting on the floor. If a passenger violates the rule of law prohibiting spitting, the conductor will call the attention of the passenger to the law prohibiting such conduct, and endeavor to persuade passenger to desist.

65. Get Witnesses—In case of ejectment, always get names of witnesses, and make report showing all the circumstances, the same as in case of accident.

66. Where to Eject—Any person ejected from a car must be put off at a regular stopping place.

No passenger will be put off at a point where likely to be exposed to danger.

Particular attention must be paid to this rule during bad and inclement weather, late at night, or when a passenger is intoxicated.

FARES AND TRANSFERS

67. Collection of Fares—Conductor must call passengers attention to the denomination of all monies tendered for fare. This will avoid mistakes. Fares must be collected promptly after passenger has boarded car. When more than one passenger or party boards car at a time the fares must be rung up on the register in the presence of the party who paid for it before any more fares are collected. Conductor must

BUILDER'S PHOTO of combination car No. 32 which with No. 34 of the same type ran on the Charleston line for many years.

Transfers ISSUED ONLY UPON REQUEST AT TIME FARE IS PAID.

Good only in continuous direction on next connecting car from point of transfer after time punched. NOT TRANSFERABLE

182003   Cond'r No.

GLOBE TICKET COMPANY, PHILA., PA.

BANGOR RAILWAY & ELECTRIC CO.

| DATE | 1 | 2 | 3 | 4 | 5 | 6 | 7 | 8 | 9 | 10 | 11 | 12 | 13 | 14 | 15 | 16 |
| | 17 | 18 | 19 | 20 | 21 | 22 | 23 | 24 | 25 | 26 | 27 | 28 | 29 | 30 | 31 | |

| HOUR | 1 | 2 | 3 | 4 | 5 | 6 | 7 | 8 | 9 | 10 | 11 | 12 |
| | 5 | 10 | 15 | 20 | 25 | 30 | 35 | 40 | 45 | 50 | 55 | 60 |

A. M. / P. M. — BREWER / CENTER / HAMMOND / HIGHLANDS / CHARLESTON / MAIN / STATE / GARLAND / EMERGENCY

ring up each fare from the place where he collects it. Thus, a fare paid inside of car must be rung up from the inside, or from the platform if collected therefrom.

In making any collection of fares after the first the conductor must call FARES distinctly.

68. Change — When necessary to give change, conductors must first register fare, and immediately thereafter give change.

69. Register Rings — Conductors must be careful to see that register rings each fare and that dial shows it.

70. Register Out of Order—In case the register gets out of order the conductor must stop using it, make report of fares on back of trip report or on blanks supplied for that purpose, and report the fact to the first inspector or starter met on the road, and subsequently report to the superintendent.

71. Transfers in Blockades—In case any line is blocked it is the desire of the company to carry passengers to their destination on other lines. Under such circumstances conductors of parallel or intersecting lines will accept transfer tickets accordingly and will issue a transfer on a transfer if necessary. They will also accept transfer passengers without tickets on orders from any inspector or authorized representative of the company, making report of same on back of trip report.

72. Persons Stealing Rides — Any person caught stealing a ride on a car must never be pushed from the car, or so frightened that he will jump while the car is in motion.

73. Thunder Storms—During thunder storms turn on the light circuit.

74. Doors Closed on Double Track—Doors must be kept closed on the double track side of car until the single track is reached.

75. Know-Nothing Stops — Know-nothing stops will be made at the following places. The car must be brought to a full stop. The conductor must not give two bells to start the car until after the car has come to a stop.

On Main Street south of the Union Street Cross-walk at the Bangor House, when bound for West Market Square.

At the top of Hammond Street Hill at the Seminary steps.

At the top of Union Street Hill near Second Street.

At the Sub-station on Park Street.

At the top of Cumberland Street Hill at Market Street.

At the foot of Cumberland Street Hill before turning onto Harlow Street.

Cars inbound on Central Street, at Warren's crossing.

Inbound cars at Brewer Junction.

On the Oldtown Division at the top of Ferry Hill.

At all steam road crossings cars must come to a full stop. Never proceed until given the signal by the flagman.

Hampden Division, north and southbound, at the Tin Bridge.

At the crossing at Cumberland and Center Streets, all cars going in either direction will come to a full stop. Car going into West Market Square from Garland Street will have the right of way over the Center Street cars going in either direction. The Center Street car going in either direction will have the right of way over the Garland Street car outbound from West Market Square.

FAILURE TO MAKE KNOW-NOTHING STOPS WILL BE DEEMED SUFFICIENT CAUSE FOR DISMISSAL.

76. Block Signals—Conductors and motormen must be careful to keep in touch with the Special Notices brought out from time to time in relation to the operation of Block Signals.

The Bucksport Branch

AT THE TIME when a charter had been procured for a proposed trolley line from Ellsworth to Bar Harbor, the Bangor newspapers printed a report that the Bangor Railway & Electric Co. was considering purchase of the Bucksport Branch of the Maine Central Railroad so as to electrify it and operate their cars over it, thus connecting with the proposed road to Bar Harbor.

The line to Bar Harbor was never built, nor were any comments published regarding the feelings of Maine Central Railroad officials toward this venture.

It is interesting, however, to consider that the original line from Bangor to Bucksport had been built in broad gauge and leased to the European & North American Railroad in 1874. Five years later that company gave up its lease and the road was taken over by new owners who narrowed the gauge to 3 feet.

In 1883 it was merged with the Maine Central and once more the gauge was changed — this time to standard.

It appears to have been a road of many changes, and its conversion to a trolley line would have been but one more for the book!

Transfer Points | **Transfers issued only upon request at time fare is paid.**

STATE & EXCHANGE to / UNION & MAIN / HAMMOND & UNION / OTIS & STATE / CUMBERLAND & HARLOW / BREWER JCT. / WEST MARKET SQ.

Good only for person to whom issued if presented at transfer point on first connecting car to destination indicated, after time and on date canceled. Continuous Trip Transfer. Not good for Stop-over. Subject to rules of Company.

344516   Cond'r No.

BANGOR RAILWAY & ELECTRIC CO.

| DATE | 1 | 2 | 3 | 4 | 5 | 6 | 7 | 8 | 9 | 10 | 11 | 12 | 13 | 14 | 15 | 16 |
| | 17 | 18 | 19 | 20 | 21 | 22 | 23 | 24 | 25 | 26 | 27 | 28 | 29 | 30 | 31 | |

| HOUR | 1 | 2 | 3 | 4 | 5 | 6 | 7 | 8 | 9 | 10 | 11 | 12 |
| | 5 | 10 | 15 | 20 | 25 | 30 | 35 | 40 | 45 | 50 | 55 | 60 |

A. M. / P. M. — BREWER / CENTER / HAMMOND / HIGHLANDS / CHARLESTON / MAIN / STATE / GARLAND / EMERGENCY

A Listing of All Car Stops on the Bangor System. . .

BANGOR RAILWAY & ELECTRIC COMPANY issued its employees, in addition to a "Book of Rules and Regulations," a 32-page pocket booklet of "Instructions to Railway Employees in Regard to Streets and General Information."

Every car stop on the Bangor system is listed and the ones the conductor was supposed to call on each trip are noted.

Such detailed information in readily available form has not survived for posterity from very many street railway operations; in many cases it probably never was written down at all by the company.

The material from this pocket-size booklet is therefore being printed in its entirety on the following pages as a significant record of Bangor's trolley days:

CITY DIVISION

CENTER STREET LOOP

Signs must read "CENTER STREET."

Register must be turned back to cipher.

When leaving Fourth & Union Streets for Center Street, if on closed car side door on left hand side must be closed and if on open car guard rail must be lowered on left hand side. Upon reaching corner of State and Exchange Street open door or lift guard rail.

When leaving State and Exchange Street for Hammond Street, close door or lower guard rail on left hand side of car, and open door or lift guard rail upon reaching Fourth and Union Streets.

Call Stop At
Norway Rd. (End of Line)
Fourteenth St. & Royal Rd.
Boutelle Road
Dean and West Sts.
Waldron's crossing
East and North Sts.
Thirteenth & Allen Sts.

Webster Ave.
Bowdoin St.
Vernon St.
West Broadway
Seventh St.
Park Crossing
Cedar & Sixth Sts. ("Know Nothing Stop")
Fifth St.
Lowder
Transfer point (Highland car) — Fourth & Union Sts.
Clinton & Third Sts.
Sanford St.
Colonial Hotel
"Know Nothing Stop" ——— Second & High Sts.
Transfer point ——— Union & Main Sts.
Water St.
Cross St.
Transfer point, regular stop —— West Market Square Waiting Room and transfer station, this car goes Center Street.
Old Post Office site
State & Exchange St. (East side)
Post Office
Tarratine Club
Penobscot St.
(Switch) ——— Somerset St.
Spring & Center St. Ave.
Transfer point (Main or Garland St. car) — Cumberland St. ("Know Nothing Stop")
Garland St.
South Park St.
Jefferson St.
Blackstone & West Park Sts.
Madison St.
McKinley St.
Congress St.
Montgomery St.
Paine Hospital
Broadway crossing
French St. crossing
Linden St.
Change signs to read "HAMMOND ST." ——— Center & Poplar Sts.
Grant St.
Norfolk St.
Poplar & Leighton Sts.
Linden St.
White's Crossing
Montgomery St.

THROUGH THE FIELDS as it looked on the Westland Avenue line when Charles Duncan shot this view on June 29, 1936. This track, which tied together the Highlands line (Ohio Street) and the Hammond Street line in a big loop, did not become part of the Bangor trolley system until 1922. (It is not included in the Book of Instructions reproduced on this and following pages.) In 1940 this locale became the site of Bangor's Dow Air Force Base and warplanes took the place of the trolley cars.

CENTER STREET LOOP—Continued.

Leighton & Congress Sts.
Congress & Fountain Sts.
Madison St.
Blackstone St.
Jefferson & Prentice Sts.
Leighton St.
Norfolk & Division Sts.
Jefferson & Center Sts.
South Park St.
Garland St.
Cumberland St. ("Know Nothing Stop")
Center St. Ave. & Spring St.
Somerset St. (Switch) ("Know Nothing Stop")
Penobscot St.
Tarratine Club
Post Office ("Know Nothing Stop")

Transfer point ———— State & Exchange Sts. ("Know Nothing Stop")
Old Post Office site

Regular stop ———— Hammond St. Waiting Room & Transfer station, car goes Hammond St.

Regular stop ———— West Market Square (Transfer point)
Cross St.
Water St.

Transfer point ———— Main & Union Sts.
Second & High Sts.
Colonial Hotel
Sanford St.
Clinton & Third Sts. (Block Signal)

Transfer point ———— Fourth & Union Sts. (Block Signal)
Lowder
Fifth St.
Cedar & Sixth Sts.
Park crossing
Seventh St.
West Broadway
Vernon St.
Bowdoin St.
Webster Ave.
Thirteenth & Allen Sts.
East & North Sts.
Waldron's Crossing
Dean & West Sts.
Boutelle Rd.
Fourteenth St. & Royal Rd.

(Change signs to read "CENTER ST.") Turn register back to ciphers.———— Norway Rd. (End of Line)

STATE STREET LOOP

From Tin Bridge to Birch Hill via Main St., Cumberland, Essex, Garland, State, Oak, Washington, Exchange, Harlow, Central, Main, Union, Hudson and Ohio St.

When leaving Thatcher St. close side door on left hand side of car. Open side door when reaching Waiting Room at corner of Central and Harlow Sts. Close side door on left hand side of car when leaving corner of Otis and State Sts. and open side door when reaching junction of Fourth and Hammond Sts. on Union St. Be governed by this same rule when open cars are in use, in place of side doors lower or lift guard rails.

Call Stop At
Thatcher St.
Dillingham St.
Car House
City Farm
Catell St.
March St.
Dutton St.
Emerson St.
Buck St.
Lincoln St.
Larkin St.
Sydney St.
Walter St.
Patten St.
Gas Works
Railroad, Parker & Davis Sts., Trunk Factory (Parkhurst's)
Cedar St.
May St.

("Know Nothing Stop"), transfer point ———— Union St. (Bangor House)
Water St.
Cross St.

Regular stop here, transfer point West Market Square
Regular stop here, transfer point Hammond St. (Transfer Station, change for Hammond and Center St. cars.)

Frey's Cafe
Old Post Office site

Regular stop ———— Waiting Room & Transfer Station. This car for Garland St. (Block Signal)
Franklin St.
High School
Spring St.
Harlow & Cumberland Sts. (Block Signal)
Market St.

("Know Nothing Stop") ———— Center St.
French St.
Broadway
Pine St. (Block Signal) (switch)
Cumberland & Essex Sts. (Block Signal)
Essex & Garland Sts.
Grove St.
Elm St.
Forest Ave.
Palm St.
Parkview Ave.
Maple St.
Birch St.
Fern St.
Pearl St.
Fruit St.

Change sign here to read "HIGHLANDS"———— Garland & Otis Sts.
Otis St. Center

Transfer point (to Old Town cars) ———— Otis & State Sts. (Block Signal)
Fruit St.
Pearl St.
Fern & East Summer Sts.
Birch St.
Wingate Ct. & Merrimac St.
Maple St.
Parkview Ave. & Newbury St.
Palm & Brown Sts.
Forest Ave. & Boyd St.
Grove & Adams Sts.
Essex St.
Pine St.
Broadway & Oak St.
All Souls Church
York St.
Hancock St.

Transfer point (change for Brewer cars) ———— Brewer Junction
Union Station
Palace Theater
Hancock St. (Penobscot Exchange Hotel)
Bijou Theeater
York St.

Transfer point (cars stop here to allow passengers to get off, but do not stop to take on passengers) ———— State & Exchange Sts.

Regular stop ———— Waiting Room and Transfer Station
Old Post Office site
Frey's Cafe

Regular stop ———— Hammond St. Transfer Station, change for Hammond and Center St. cars.

Transfer point, regular stop ———— West Market Square
Cross St.
Water St.
Main & Union Sts.
Second & High Sts.
Colonial Hotel
Sanford St.
Clinton & Third Sts.

Transfer point (Hammond St. car) ———— Fourth & Hammond Sts. (Block Signal)
Union & Hudson Sts.
Hudson & Ohio Sts.
Chatham St. (switch) (Block Signal)
George St.
Everett St.
Highland Ave.
Charles & Court Sts.
Bower St.
James St.
Smith St.
Autumn St.
Winter & Jackson Sts.
Cottage & Fremont Sts.
Kossuth St.
Wiley & Holland Sts.
Currier's crossing
Fourteenth St.
Quimby's crossing
Fifteenth St.
Sixteenth St.

Change signs to read "STATE ST." ———— Seventeenth St. (End of line Birch Hill)

STATE STREET LOOP

From Birch Hill to Tin Bridge via Ohio, Hudson, Union, Main, Central, Harlow, Exchange, Washington, Oak, State, Otis, Garland, Essex, Cumberland, Harlow, Central and Main St.

Register must be turned back to ciphers when leaving Birch Hill.

When leaving Fourth & Hammond Sts. on Union St., close side door on left hand side, if on closed car, or lower guard rail if on open car; and open door, or lift guard rail when reaching corner of State and Otis Sts.

When leaving Waiting Room at Graham Bldg., close side door on left hand side, or lower guard rail; and open door or lift guard rail when leaving double iron at Thatcher St.

Call Stop at
Sixteenth St.
Fifteen St.
Quimby's crossing
Fourteenth St.
Currier's crossing
Wiley & Holland Sts.
Kossuth St.
Cottage & Fremont Sts.
Winter & Jackson Sts.
Autumn St.
Smith St.
James St.
Bower St.
Charles & Court Sts.
Highland Ave.
Everett St.
George St.
Chatham St. (block signal) (switch)
Ohio & Hudson Sts.
Hudson & Union Sts.

Transfer point (Hammond St. Cars) —— Fourth & Hammond Sts. (block signal)
Clinton & Third Sts.
Sanford St.
Colonial Hotel
"Know Nothing Stop" —— Second & High Sts.
Transfer point —— Union & Main Sts.
Water St.
Cross St.
Transfer point, regular stop —— West Market Square
Regular stop —— Hammond St. Transfer Station, change for Hammond & Center St. cars.
Frey's Cafe
Old Post Office site
Regular stop —— Waiting Room and Transfer Station

Transfer point, "Know Nothing Stop" —— State and Exchange Sts.
York St.
Bijou Theater
Hancock St. (Penobscot Exchange Hotel)
Palace Theater
Union Station
Transfer point for Brewer cars— Brewer Junction
Hanock St.
York St.
All Souls Church
Broadway
Pine St.
Essex St.
Grove & Adams Sts.
Forest Ave. & Boyd St.
Palm & Brown Sts.
Parkview Ave. & Newbury St.
Maple St.
Wingate Ct. & Merrimac St.
Birch St.
Fern & East Summer Sts.
Pearl St.
Fruit St.
State & Otis Sts. (Block signal)
Otis St. Center
Change signs to read "MAIN ST." —— Otis & Garland Sts.
Fruit St.
Pearl St.
Fern St.
Birch St.
Maple St.
Parkview Ave.
Palm St.
Forest Ave.
Elm St.
Grove St.
Garland & Essex Sts.
Essex & Cumberland Sts. (Block signal) (switch)
Pine St. (Block signal)
Broadway
French St.
"Know Nothing Stop" —— Center St.
"Know Nothing Stop" —— Market St.
"Know Nothing Stop" —— Cumberland & Harlow Sts. (Block signal)
Spring St.
High school
Franklin St.
Regular stop —— Waiting Room & Transfer Station, car goes to Main St.
Old Post Office site

RIVERSIDE PARK — Trolley station at once-famous summer park on a spur off the Hampden line two fares out of Bangor.

STATE STREET LOOP—Continued

Frey's Cafe

"Know Nothing Stop" ——————— Hammond St. Transfer Station, change for Hammond and Center St. cars

Regular stop ——————— West Market Square, transfer point
Cross St.
Water St.

Transfer point ——————— Union St. (Bangor House)
May St.
Cedar St.
Trunk Factory (Parkhurst's)
Railroad, Parker & Davis Sts.
Gas Works
Patten St.
Walter St.
Sidney St.
Larkin St.
Lincoln St.
Buck St.
Emerson St.
Dutton St.
March St.
Catell St.
City Farm
Car House
Dilingham St.
Thatcher St.
End of route at Tin Bridge

HAMPDEN DIVISION

Register must be turned back to ciphers when car leaves Post Office Square for Hampden and again at Stearn's Mill, Hampden Highlands and end of line, also signs must read "HAMPDEN."

Signs must read "BANGOR" on car leaving Hampden, end of line; and register must be turned back to ciphers at Hampden Highlands, and at Frost's switch.

When leaving P. O. Square, conductor will call the following stops unless marked with star:

*Old Post Office site
*Frey's Cafe

"Know Nothing Stop" ——————— Hammond St. Transfer Station, change for Hammond & Center St. cars

(Transfer Point) Regular stop — West Market Square
Cross St.
Water St.

"Know Nothing Stop" when running from Hampden to Bangor — Union St.
May St.
Cedar St.

TROLLEY WAITING SHELTER—The Dorothea Dix Park former trolley station in Hampden looked like this in 1970.

Trunk Factory (Parkhurst's)
Railroad, Parker & Davis Sts.
Gas Works
Patten St.
Walter St.
Sydney St.
Larkin St.
Lincoln St.
Buck St.
*Fair Grounds or Auditorium
Emerson St.
Dutton St.
March St.
Catell St.
City Farm
Dillingham St.

Close left hand side door or lower left hand guard rail here, when running Hampden to Bangor. Open door or lift guard rail, when running Bangor to Hampden. ——————— Thatcher St.

"Know Nothing Stop" both directions ——————— Tin Bridge
*Courcy Residence
*Limit Pole
*Back Road
*Mason Residence
Engel's Mill
Hunting Store
Kelley's Lane
*Waters Residence
*Foley's
*Lucy Residence
Leary's switch
*Quirk Residence
*Prout's Residence
Stearn's Mill
*Bolton Residence
*Waters Residence
*York Residence
*Gilmore Residence
*Lynn Residence
*Dillingham Residence
*Hardy's Path
*Ray Residence
*Moore Residence
*Wyman Residence
*Bartlett Bungalow
*Bartlett House

End of 1st Fare Limit Bangor to Hampden ——————— *Hodgkins House
Frost's Switch
*Clark Residence
*Lander's Residence
*Holland Residence
*Twaddel Residence
*Carver Residence
*Nason Residence
*Burn's Residence
*Whitmore Residence
*Rollins Residence
Riverside Park (Switches)
*Flynn Residence
*Mrs. Stearn's Residence
*Louis Stearns
Emerson's Store
*Grist Mill
Elm St.
*Cookson Residence
*Norris Switch
*Blanchard Residence

Regular Stop ——————— Hampden (Upper Corner)
*Fessenden Residence
Cottage Street
*Hewes Residence
*Odd Fellows Hall
Town Hall
*Cemetery
*Jewett Residence
*Reed's Hollow
*Cole Residence
*Rev. Humphrey's Residence
*Swett's Stable

Regular Stop, End of 2nd Fare Limit Bangor to Hampden; End of First Fare Limit Hampden to Bangor ——————— Hampden Highlands (Lower Corner)
*Snow Residence
*Mayo Residence
*Gilbert Residence
*Flagg Residence
*Nickerson Residence
*Carver Residence
Dorothea Dix Park
*Millett Residence
*Plummer Residence
*Emerson Residence (End of Line)

When running from Hampden to Bangor, conductor will call stops in reverse order.

CHARLESTON DIVISION

Leaving Post Office Square for Charleston, register must be turned back to ciphers and conductor will call out stops at the following places marked with a star:

Regular Stop —————————
*State & Exchange Sts.
*Old Post Office site
*Transfer Station change for Hammond & Center St. cars
*Frey's Cafe
Old Post Office site

Regular Stop —————————
*Waiting Room & Transfer Station, car goes to Charleston (Block signal)
*Franklin St.
*High School
*Spring St. (Block signal)

Transfer point (inbound) —————————
*Cumberland St. (Block signal)
*Curve St.
*Kenduskeag Ave.
Morse & Co.'s Mill
Morse's Bridge

Side Track —————————
(Block signals)
Holland St.
Maxfield's Bridge
Grant's Tannery
Clark Residence

"Know Nothing Stop" in both directions —————————
Side track to Eaton's Mill (Block signals)

"Know Nothing Stop" when running from Charleston to Bangor —————————
Bruce Road (Eaton's Grist Mill)
Ice Houses
Morrill Residence
Berry Residence
Barker Residence
Perkins Residence

Isaac Jordan Residence
L. A. Strout Residence
Burnham Residence
Kenduskeag & Valley Ave.
George Weiler Residence
Samuel Strout Residence
Pettingill Residence
*Strickland Road

9th Fare Limit, Charleston to Bangor —————————
*Griffin Road
Jake Weiler Residence
Bertha Weiler Residence
Frost's Residence
Thomas Residence
*Tuberculosis Hospital
Jordan's Residence (Block signals)

1st Fare Limit, Bangor to Charleston —————————
Frost's (Buckley's siding)
Merritt Weiler Residence
*Broadway Crossing
*Bean's Store
*Dudley Hill
Newcomb Farm (B. R. & E. Co. Farm)

8th Fare Limit, Charleston to Bangor Switch —————————
Side track to Six Mile Falls Potato House and to Gravel Pit
Orr Residence
George Graves Residence
*Six Mill Falls
*Finson Rd. & Coyt Residence

2nd Fare Limit Side Track, Bangor to Charleston —————————
*North Bangor, B.&A. R.R. Sta.
Fred Getchell's
*McCarthy Road
Cluff place

13-BENCH OPEN CAR No. 13 is shown on the Hampden line in June 1912. Three cars of this type were purchased that year from the Laconia Car Co. to handle the heavy riding that had developed on the Hampden line and to popular Riverside Park.

CHARLESTON DIVISION—Continued

	Brown place
7th Fare Limit, Charleston to Bangor	Charles Bragg Residence
3rd Fare Limit Bangor to Charleston	Wentworth's Siding McDonald Residence Berry Residence Worcester's Bridge
6th Fare Limit, Charleston to Bangor	*Glenburn Center Road Worcester's Farm (Worcester's Siding) Barney place Black's Siding
4th Fare Limit, Bangor to Charleston	*Black's Farm
5th Fare Limit, Charleston to Bangor	Frank Smith's Residence Haskell Residence (Switch)
Regular Stop	*Waiting Room, Kenduskeag (Switch)
Regular Stop	*Post Office Spratt Residence Towle Residence Harvey Residence (Foss' Siding)
5th Fare Limit, Bangor to Charleston	Foster Road Fitz Residence Nason Residence William Smith Residence Walter Smith Residence Glidden Residence Holt Residence Wilson's Waiting Room Freeze Residence
4th Fare Limit, Charleston to Bangor	*Higginsville Siding
6th Fare Limit, Bangor to Charleston	Genesis Residence Maise Residence Frawley Residence Albert Whitney Residence
3rd Fare Limit, Charleston to Bangor	Tyler Farm Gould Residence Corson Residence Beech Grove Casino *Houston Residence Houston's Siding Willey Residence
7th Fare Limit, Bangor to Charleston	Hawes Residence Cedar Valley Lumber Co. Ervin Rider Residence Frank Foster Residence Fred Hinckley Residence Charles Chandler Residence Oscar Duren Residence White School House Charles Palmer Residence Lewellyn Duren Residence Duren Residence Ernest Page Residence Ralph Smith Residence Beane Residence Soule Residence Frank Everett Residence
2nd Fare Limit, Charleston to Bangor	Graham Farm Henry Everett Residence Tilton Residence Nickerson Residence Whittier Residence Ventry House W. E. Bagley Residence Brown House John Barker Residence F. W. Hill Residence Annette Residence Gerald Residence Dr. Schofield Residence Fred Hill Residence East Corinth Freight Shed (Switches) *Ripley's Stable *Post Office
Regular Stop	*Waiting Room, East Corinth Morrison Ave. Albert Shaw's Residence Annie Herrick Residence Tozier Residence Chandler Residence Collins Residence A. P. Brown Residence Brown's Siding Frank Everett's Residence
8th Fare Limit, Bangor to Charleston	Maine Packing Co. Siding East Corinth Creamery Patterson Residence

	Fred Bickmore Residence John Whitney Residence Tiplady Residence Lawton Residence Jenkins Residence Leila Whitney Residence Brooks Residence Strout Residence Foote Residence Marshall Residence Wesley Foss Residence Ripley's Siding Charles Perkin's Residence Hiram Foss Residence
9th Fare Limit, Bangor to Charleston	Williams Mill Siding
1st Fare Limit, Charleston to Bangor	Clapham Residence Turner Residence Warton Residence Williams Residence Simpson Potato House (Siding) *Four Corners Charleston Creamery George Russell Residence Toby Residence Robinson Residence Goss Residence Mitchell Residence Grange Hall Emery Residence Elden Residence Scribner Residence McLellan Residence Higgins Classical Institute Dormitory Mrs. Higgins Residence Dr. Weymouth Residence
Regular Stop	*Farmers Store Stocker Residence P. A. Bennett Residence Frank Bickmore Residence End of Line at Charleston

Conductor will call stops when running Charleston to Bangor in reverse order to that from Bangor to Charleston.

BREWER DIVISION

When leaving Post Office Square register must be turned back to cipher and signs must read "BREWER."

Call Stops at:

"Know Nothing Stop"	State & Exchange Sts. York St. Bijou Theater Hancock St. (Penobscot Exchange Hotel) Palace Theater Union Station Brewer Junction
"Know Nothing Stop" in both directions	Pine St.
Regular stop in both directions	Merrill's Corner Center & North Main Sts. Parker St. Church St. Union St.
Regular stop in both directions	Wilson St. Brimmer St. School St. Spring St. (Switch) Maple St. Burr St. Oak Hill (cemetery) Wilson Residence Dyer's Cove Getchell Farm Abbott St. Three twenty six Grove St. McCoy St. Pendleton St. Patten St. Tibbets & Harris Sts. Ayer's store King's Court Derusha Lane
"Know Nothing Stop" in both directions	Eastern Mfg. Co. crossing Brewer St. Post Office Sargent's Mill Elm St. End of Line, South Brewer

Register must be turned to cipher when leaving end of line at South Brewer for Bangor and stops called in reverse order to that from Bangor to Brewer, until arriving at State & Exchange Sts., when car goes via State, Hammond and Central Sts. to Post Office Square. After leaving corner of State & Exchange Sts., conductor will call the following places:

Regular stop ———————
Old Post Office site
Transfer Station for Hammond & Center St. cars
Frey's Cafe
Old Post Office site
Waiting Room & Transfer Station, car goes to Brewer.

OLD TOWN DIVISION

Sign must read "OLD TOWN" when leaving Post Office Square and remain so until arriving at end of line at Great Works, when it will be turned to read "BANGOR."

When leaving Post Office Square, Bangor, register must be turned back to ciphers; arriving at School St., Veazie, register must be turned back, and also at Island Ave. in Orono.

When leaving end of line at Great Works, register must be turned back to ciphers, and again it must be turned back when arriving at Grave's residence in Orono, and at Veazie Hill switch.

Call stops at the following places unless marked with star: Post Office Square, Waiting Room and Transfer Station, car goes to Old Town. (Regular Stop).

Call Stops At

"Know Nothing Stop," transfer point ———————
State & Exchange Sts.
York St.
Bijou Theater
Hancock St. (Penobscot Exchange Hotel)
Palace Theater
Union Station
Brewer Junction

Transfer point ———————
"Know Nothing Stop" here when running from Great Works to Bangor.

Hancock St.
York St.
All Souls Church
Oak St. & Broadway
Pine St.
Essex St.
Grove & Adams Sts.
Forest Ave. & Boyd St.
Palm & Brown Sts.
Parkview Ave. & Newbury St.
Maple St.
Wingate Ct. & Merrimac St.

Transfer point. Open left hand side door when running from Bangor to Great Works. Close left hand side door when running from Great Works to Bangor. ———————

Birch St.
Fern & East Summer Sts.
Pearl St.
Fruit St.

Otis St. (Block signal)
Howard St.
Bellevue Ave.
Summit Ave. & Eastern Maine General Hospital (Block Signal)
Water Works Switch. (Block signal)
Water Works
State Hospital
Hogan Road
*Dr. Peter's residence
*Golf Club
*Gilbert residence
*Granite Works
Mt. Hope, Lower Gate (Block signal)
*Mt. Hope switch (Block signal)
Mt. Hope Upper Gate
*Mt. Hope Ave.
*Veazie Gravel Pit
*Weed's Garage
*Landy residence
*Lyford residence
School St.
*Canoe Factory
*Hersey residence
*Jones' Farm

Regular stop ———————
Veazie
Lemon St.
*Johnson residence
*Elm Tree
*Spencer residence
*Maine Central Railroad Crossing ("Know Nothing Stop" here in both directions)
*McPheter's residence
*Calkin residence
*Barney Silver residence
*Barney Gass residence
*Andrew Smith residence
*Fred Hathorn residence
*Harrison Page residence

WHEN A TOURING CAR disputed the right-of-way with a fast-moving semi-convertible in the 1920s, it came out second best.

OLD TOWN DIVISION—Continued

	*Nathan Page residence
	Gardner Road
	*Brown residence
	*Perkins Farm
	*Ayer Farm
	Kelley Road
	*Bennock residence
	*Bennock's switch (Block signals)
	*Page residence
	*Estes residence
	*Hillside Villa
	*Andrew McPheters residence
	*Scott residence
	Island Ave. (or Basin Mills)
	*Gilbert residence
	Hamlin St.
	*Hamlin residence
	High School
	*Estabrook residence
	*Dr. Mayo's residence
	Juniper St. (Catholic Church)
	*Dr. Whitcomb's residence
Regular stop ————	Orono Waiting Room
"Know Nothing Stop" ————	Mill St.
(When running from Bangor to Great Works)	
	North Main St. (Webster)
	*Sigma Chi House (and Webster's residence)
	Park St.
	*Prof. Davie residence
	*Shaw residence
	*Shaw's switch
	*Dean Hart's residence
	Lambda Chi Alpha House
	Phi Kappa Sigma House
	Phi Gamma Delta House
	Mt. Vernon (Phi Eta Kappa, Kappa Sigma, Delta Tau Delta
(Block signal) ————	
Regular stop both directions ——	University Waiting Room (S.A.E. House)
	Beta House (Hannibal Hamlin Hall)
	Theta Chi House
	North Hall
	*Graves residence
	*Chrysler's residence
	*Briscoe's residence & Spearing Inn
	*Craig residence
	*Patch residence
	Vacant

	*Folsom's residence
	*Storman's residence
(Block signal) ————	*Buck's switch
	*Woodward residence
Regular stop in both directions—	Stillwater Corner
	*Wickett residence
	*Cloverdale Cemetery
	*Spencer & Leavitt's residence
	*Mishou's residence (House on the rock)
	*Thibedeau residence
	*Potter's Milk Farm
	*Abbott residence
	*Smith residence
(Block signal) ————	Hospital switch
	*White & Loud's residence
	Hospital
	Center St.
	Gamon's Crossing
	Carbarn
	Elm St.
	Veazie St.
	Fourth St.
	High St.
	Brunswick St.
Regular stop in both directions---	Indian Ferry & Boutin's Corner
	*Boulieu Bros.
	*Old Town Tea Store
	Middle St.
Regular stop ————	Waiting Room
Regular stop ————	Old Town stop
"Know Nothing Stop" when running from Great Works to Bangor ————	
	*Strand Theater
	*Bickmore Gall Cure or Sawyer's
	Willow St. or Station
	*Jordan's
	Catholic Church
	Carroll St.
	Pine St.
	Eaton St.
	Congress St.
	Cooper St.
	*Jarvis Store
	*Moran's
	*Chas. Smith & Henry Shaw
	*Grady residence
	*Carrow residence
	*Catholic Cemetery
	*Top of hill
	Jameson St.
Turn signs to read "BANGOR"	(End of line Great Works)

Conductor will call stops from Great Works to Bangor in the reverse order of that from Bangor to Great Works.

A Few Words About the Author of Bangor Street Railway ...

CHARLES D. HESELTINE was born almost within the shadow of the Munjoy Hill carbarn in the city of Portland, Maine. His early years were spent playing within and being chased out of this carbarn as related in the article "Carbarn Kids" printed in the July, 1953, issue of Railroad Magazine. At the age of nine he was taking pictures of the cars with a Brownie box camera. This has continued as a life-long hobby.

In the late 'Thirties came an offer to break in as a motorman on the Portland system, as he had frequently handled cars in and around the local barns in an unofficial capacity and he was given the opportunity to run one of the Birney cars to the end of the Thornton Heights line for transfer to the Biddeford & Saco Railroad via flatbed trailer.

However, at the same time he was in receipt of a notice of his forthcoming appointment to the local fire department and, with some regret, felt that this offered a better economic future than trolley operating. Consequently, he served out his time as a fire-fighter and became City Sealer of Weights & Measures, retiring in 1966. The following day he joined the staff of the Maine Historical Society as a custodian, a post he continues to hold.

Mr. Heseltine has specialized in pictures and histories of the electric lines of the state of Maine and has pictures of each of the 58 operating companies of the Pine Tree State. Also, he is much in demand to speak before service clubs, lodges, old peoples' groups and others on "trolleyism."

WEEKLY PASS in use by the successor Penobscot Transportation Co. during wartime years of 1940-1945 when it operated Bangor's city trolley lines.

Reproduction of a 1914 Bangor Trolley Timetable from the Collection of J. R. McFarlane.

TIME TABLE
FOR ALL LINES OF THE

Bangor Railway & Electric Co.

In Effect SEPT. 28, 1914.
Subject to change without notice.

CARS FROM HAMMOND ST. run to Center St.

CARS FROM CENTER ST. run to Hammond St.

CARS FROM OHIO ST. run to State St. and via Garland and Main Sts. to the Tin Bridge.

CARS FROM MAIN ST. run to Garland St. and via State and Ohio Sts. to Birch Hill.

CARS FROM STATE ST. run to Ohio St.

CARS FROM GARLAND ST. run to Main St.

**L. H. THOMPSON, Printer,
Brewer**

BREWER DIV.

Leave W. Market Sq. Bangor, for South Brewer		Leave South Brewer for W. Market Sq. Bangor	
A.M.	P.M.	A.M.	P.M.
z 5.20	12.20	z 5.40	12.20
z 5.40	12.40	z 6.00	12.40
z 6.00	1.00	z 6.20	1.00
z 6.20	1.20	z 6.40	1.20
z 6.40	1.40	z 7.00	1.40
7.00	2.00	7.20	2.00
7.20	2.20	7.40	2.20
7.40	2.40	8.00	2.40
8.00	3.00	8.20	3.00
8.20	3.20	8.40	3.20
8.40	3.40	9.00	3.40
9.00	4.00	9.20	4.00
9.20	4.20	9.40	4.20
9.40	4.40	10.00	4.40
10.00	5.00	10.20	5.00
10.20	5.20	10.40	5.20
10.40	5.40	11.00	5.40
11.00	6.00	11.20	6.00
11.20	6.20	11.40	6.20
11.40	6.40	12.00	6.40
12.00	7.00		7.00
	7.20		7.20
	7.40		7.40
	8.00		8.00
	8.20		8.20
	8.40		8.40
	9.00		9.00
	9.20		9.20
	9.40		9.40
	10.00		10.00
	10.20		10.20
	10.40		10.40
	11.00		11.00
	11.20		11.20
			11.40

zNot run Sundays.

CITY LINES

Leave Otis St. for West Market Square via State St.

6.04, 6.34, 7.04, 7.34, 8.04, 8.34, 9.04, 9.19, 9.34 and 9.49 a. m. and every 15 minutes up to 9.04 p. m. After 9.04 p. m. leave 9.34, 10.04, 10.34 and 11.04 p. m.

CITY LINES
CARS LEAVE WEST MARKET SQ.

For Hammond and Center Sts		For State St. and Highlands		For Garland St.		For Main St.	
z5.45	12.15	z6.15	12.00	z5.55	12.10	z6.15	12.05
z6.15	12.35	z6.45	12.15	z6.25	12.25	z6.35	12.20
z6.45	12.55	7.15	12.30	z6.55	12.40	z6.45	12.35
7.15	1.15	7.45	12.45	7.25	12.55	z7.05	12.50
7.35	1.35	8.15	1.00	7.55	11.10	z7.15	1.05
7.55	1.55	8.45	1.15	8.25	1.25	7.35	1.20
8.15	2.15	9.00	1.30	8.55	1.40	8.05	1.35
8.35	2.35	9.15	1.45	9.10	1.55	8.35	1.50
8.55	2.55	9.30	2.00	9.25	2.10	8.50	2.05
9.15	3.15	9.45	2.15	9.40	2.25	9.05	2.20
9.35	3.35	10.00	2.30	9.55	2.40	9.20	2.35
9.55	3.55	10.15	2.45	10.10	2.55	9.35	2.50
10.15	4.15	10.30	3.00	10.25	3.10	9.50	3.05
10.35	4.35	10.45	3.15	10.40	3.25	10.05	3.20
10.55	4.55	11.00	3.30	10.55	3.40	10.20	3.35
11.15	5.15	11.15	3.45	11.10	3.55	10.35	3.50
11.35	5.35	11.30	4.00	11.25	4.10	10.50	4.05
11.55	5.55	11.45	4.15	11.40	4.25	11.05	4.20
	6.15		4.30	11.55	4.40	11.20	4.35
	6.35		4.45		4.55	11.35	4.50
	6.55		5.00		5.10	11.50	5.05
	7.15		5.15		5.25		5.20
	7.35		5.30		5.40		5.35
	7.55		5.45		5.55		5.50
	8.15		6.00		6.10		6.05
	8.35		6.15		6.25		6.20
	8.55		6.30		6.40		6.35
	9.15		6.45		6.55		6.50
	9.35		7.00		7.10		7.05
	9.55		7.15		7.25		7.20
	10.15		7.30		7.40		7.35
	10.35		7.45		7.55		7.50
	10.55		8.00		8.10		8.05
	11.15		8.15		8.25		8.20
			8.30		8.40		8.35
			8.45		8.55		8.50
			9.15		9.25		9.05
			9.45		9.55		9.35
			10.15		10.25		10.05
			10.45		10.55		10.35
			11.15				11.05
							11.35

z Not run Sundays.

Leave Otis St. for West Market Square via Garland St.

6.25, 6.55, 7.25, 7.55, 8.25, 8.55 a. m. and every 15 minutes up to 8.55 p. m. After 8.55 p. m. leave 9.25, 9.55, 10.25 and 10.55 p. m.

The Phantom Trolley . . .

IN THE EARLY DAYS of the street railway industry many spare carmen were recruited when traffic was heavy and many extra cars were placed in service. Among these part-time motormen and conductors were always a few not known for their caution. The slogan "Safety First" had not come into general usage and there were those who occasionally seemed more than willing to take a chance.

As related to the author, one such crew had taken a special group to attend a fraternal society function at East Corinth, laying over at the East Corinth spur into the freight house.

Ready for the return trip, the crew called the dispatcher at Bangor as, at that time, the division had not been equipped with block signals. Orders were received to meet the late outbound car at Kenduskeag Village.

As the party broke up and boarded the car sooner than anticipated, the special left East Corinth with many minutes to spare. On the front seat of the big open trolley were several gay young blades fortified with liquid spirit. Remarking about several fast runs back to Bangor, they commenced to urge the motor-man to attempt to set a new record, encouraging him to "open her up." The young spare motorman was only too happy to accept the challenge and took off from East Corinth Village like a greased goose.

The eight miles to Kenduskeag siding was covered at a fast clip, the car spinning along the level stretches and racing down the dips and hollows. Others aboard the car became affected by the spirit of the race and began chanting for more and more speed. Arriving at Kenduskeag, the car crew held a brief consultation. Watches in hand, they knew they were so far ahead of the time scheduled for the arrival of the outbound car from Bangor that they could safely run the three miles to Worster's spur and make their meet there. Wasn't the last car out of Bangor the theater car, and wasn't it usually late in getting away after the theater let out?

The conductor gave the two-bells signal and the special was off again on its wild run, the passengers screaming with glee as the wheels bit into the curves and flanges squealed. They shouted encouragement to the controller artist on the front platform, as they hurtled along.

The conductor, however, commenced to have mis-

Continued

Reproduction of a 1914 Bangor Trolley Timetable from the Collection of J. R. McFarlane.

HAMPDEN DIV.

Bangor to Hampden			Hampden to Bangor		
Leave Bangor	Leary's Switch	Frost's Switch	Leave Hampden	Leary's Switch	Frost's Switch
A.M.	A.M.	A.M.	A.M.	A.M.	A.M.
*5.10	5.23	5.28	*5.40	5.52	6.00
*5.30	5.45	5.52	*6.05	6.25	6.30
*6.15	6.30	6.37	*6.52	7.07	7.15
6.45	7.00	7.07	7.22	7.37	7.45
7.30	7.45	7.52	8.07	8.22	8.30
8.00	8.15	8.22	8.37	8.52	9.00
8.45	9.00	9.07	9.22	9.37	9.45
9.15	9.30	9.37	9.52	10.07	10.15
10.00	10.15	10.22	10.37	10.52	11.00
10.30	10.45	10.52	11.07	11.22	11.30
11.15	11.30	11.37	11.52	P.M.	P.M.
11.45	12.00	P.M.	P.M.	12.07	12.15
P.M.	P.M.	12.07	12.22	12.37	12.45
12.30	12.45	12.52	1.07	1.22	1.30
1.00	1.15	1.22	1.37	1.52	2.00
1.45	2.00	2.07	2.22	2.37	2.45
2.15	2.30	2.37	2.52	3.07	3.15
3.00	3.15	3.22	3.37	3.52	4.00
3.30	3.45	3.52	4.07	4.22	4.30
4.15	5.00	5.07	5.22	5.37	5.45
5.30	5.45	5.52	6.07	6.22	6.30
6.00	6.15	6.22	6.37	6.52	7.00
6.45	7.00	7.07	7.22	7.37	7.45
7.15	7.30	7.37	7.52	8.07	8.15
8.00	8.15	8.22	8.37	8.52	9.00
8.30	8.45	8.52	9.07	9.22	9.30
9.15	9.30	9.37	9.52	10.07	10.15
9.45	10.00	10.07	10.22	10.37	10.45
10.30	10.45	10.52	11.07	11.22	11.30
11.00	11.15	11.22	11.37	11.52	12.00

z Not run Sunday.

Sunday Special leaves Sterns' Mill at 6.45 a. m. for Bangor.

OLD TOWN DIVISION

Leave Bangor for Veazie, Orono Old Town, G. Works		Leave Great Works for Old Town, Orono Veazie and Bangor	
* 5.30	12.00	* 5.45	12.15
* 6.00	12.30	6.45	12.45
* 6.30	1.00	* 7.15	1.15
7.00	1.30	* 7.45	1.45
7.30	2.00	8.15	2.15
8.00	2.30	8.45	2.45
8.30	3.00	9.15	3.15
9.00	3.30	9.45	3.45
9.30	4.00	10.15	4.15
10.00	4.30	10.45	4.45
10.30	5.00	11.15	5.15
11.00	5.30	11.45	5.45
11.30	6.00		6.15
	6.30		6.45
	7.00		7.15
	7.30		7.45
	8.00		8.15
	8.30		8.45
	9.00		9.15
			9.45
	10.00		10.15
	11.00		11.15

*Not run Sundays.

Extra Cars on Saturday Nights.

On Saturday nights cars leave West Market Square every 15 minutes up to 11.15 p.m. for the Highlands, State St. and Main St., and every 15 minutes up to 10.55 p. m. for Garland St.

SUNDAYS.

First Trip from West Market Square.

for Hammond St., Center St., State St. and Highlands, 7.15 a. m., Garland St., 7.25 a. m. Main St., 7.35 a. m. Then same as weekdays.

Leave End of Lines.

Leave Hammond and Center Sts. at 7.25 a. m., Birch Hill on Ohio St. 7.30 a. m., Otis St. on State St., 7.34 a. m., Otis St. on Garland St., 7.25 a. m., Tin Bridge on Main St., 7.15 a. m. Then same as weekdays.

CHARLESTON DIV.

Rate of Fare	Bangor	Buckley's	Seaport Jct.	Wentworth's	Worster's	Kenduskeag	Higginsville	Houston's	East Corinth	Robbin's Mills	Charleston
Bangor		5	10	15	20	25	30	35	40	45	50
Buckley's	5		5	10	15	20	25	30	35	40	45
Seaport Jct.	10	5		5	10	15	20	25	30	35	40
Wentworth's	15	10	5		5	10	15	20	25	30	35
Worster's	20	15	10	5		5	10	15	20	25	30
Kenduskeag	25	20	15	10	5		5	10	15	20	25
Higginsville	30	25	20	15	10	5		5	10	15	20
Houston's	35	30	25	20	15	10	5		5	10	15
East Corinth	40	35	30	25	20	15	10	5		5	10
Robbin's Mills	45	40	35	30	25	20	15	10	5		5
Charleston	50	45	40	35	30	25	20	15	10	5	

Employees on Passenger Cars will NOT take charge of letters or bundles of any kind.

SPECIAL SUNDAY RATES

Bangor to Charleston and return   75c
Bangor to East Corinth and return   60c
Bangor to Kenduskeag and return   40c

Special-rate Tickets are sold at the Main St. waiting room, and are not for sale on the cars.

On week days parties of twelve or over can get the above rates by applying for same at the Main St. waiting room.

No Freight, Bicycles or Baby Carriages will be taken on Passenger Cars.

No Passengers will be taken on Freight Cars.

THE PHANTOM TROLLEY—Continued

givings and, taking a deep breath, made his precarious way along the running board of the rocking trolley to accost his running mate. Maybe they could be heading into trouble. A cornfield meet with a full carload of special riders would be difficult to explain. But, happily, there was a way out!

For a few years there was a long spur running into a lumber operation about midway between Kenduskeag and Worster's siding. It was just ahead over the next rise. Now a bit apprehensive himself, the erstwhile devil-may-care motorman eased his car down to a crawl as the conductor raced ahead to throw the switch for the lumber spur. The big car rolled into the siding several hundred feet, behind a stand of trees, the conductor realigning the switch and following on foot.

Within minutes the outbound car swooshed past, its crew intent upon making up the time lost in picking up the theater crowd and not noticing the waiting car on the spur behind the trees. The special then pulled back onto the main line and continued on to Bangor.

Arriving at Kenduskeag Village, the outbound crew stopped on the siding to await the special in accordance with orders. After a futile wait of a quarter hour or so, the conductor called the dispatcher. No word had been received of the special and the outbound car was ordered to continue on, at a cautious pace, with the expectation of finding the special somewhere in the ditch. Apparently some fearful disaster had overtaken it! However, upon reaching its terminus at East Corinth, and not sighting the "lost" car, the crew reported as much, thus creating a certain amount of uneasiness in the dispatcher's office.

Shortly afterwards, the special, having discharged its passengers in Bangor, rolled into the Main Street carbarn to put up for the night. By this time the crew felt they had the makings of a rare joke. Upon being questioned by the dispatcher, they blithely told him they had, indeed, passed the outbound car at Kenduskeag Village as ordered! The unhappy crew of the regular car were called on the carpet the following day by the superintendent and accused of being drunk while on duty. It was some days before the mystery of the "Phantom Car" was finally unravelled—enough time for it to have been established as a legend among Bangor carmen.!

Continued
Reproduction of a 1914 Bangor Trolley Timetable

CHARLESTON DIV.

Passenger Cars Leave Bangor Daily	Front St.	W. Market Sq. De.	Morse's	Buckley's	Six Mile Falls Carhouse	North Bangor Seaport Jct.	Wentworth's	Worster's	Kenduskeag	Higginsville	Houston's	East Corinth	Ripley's	Four Corners	Charleston Ar.
A.M.		†6.55	7.00	7.07	7.14	7.25									
		8.05	8.11	8.23	x8.30	8.35	8.43	8.50	x 9.00	9.10	9.20	9.33	9.41	9.52	10.00
		10.05	10.11	10.23	10.30	10.35	10.43	10.50	x11.00	11.10	11.20	11.33	11.41	11.52	12.00
P.M.		12.05	12.11	12.23	12.30	12.35	12.43	12.50	x 1.00	1.10	1.20	1.33	1.41	1.52	2.00
		2.05	2.11	2.23	2.30	2.35	2.43	2.50	x 3.00	3.10	3.20	3.33	3.41	3.52	4.00
		4.05	4.11	4.23	4.30	4.35	4.43	4.50	x 5.00	5.10	5.20	5.33	5.41	5.52	6.00
		6.05	6.11	6.23	6.30	6.35	6.43	6.50	x 7.00	7.10	7.20	7.33	7.41	7.52	8.00
Freight A.M.	11.50	12.05	12.12	12.39	12.49	12.53	1.04	z1.10	ar 1.20 de 1.35	1.55	2.05	ar z2.23 de 2.45	2.55	3.12	3.25

CHARLESTON to BANGOR

Passenger Cars Leave Charleston Daily	Charleston Lv.	Four Corners	Ripley's	East Corinth	Houston's	Higginsville	Kenduskeag	Worster's	Wentworth's	North Bangor Seaport Jct.	Six Mile Falls Carhouse	Buckley's	Morse's	W. Market Sq.	Front St.
A.M.										†7.25	7.30	7.37	7.49	7.55	
	q7.05	7.12	7.23	7.30	7.45	7.55	x 8.00	8.10	8.17	8.25	x8.30	8.37	8.49	8.55	
	10.05	10.12	10.23	10.30	10.45	10.55	x11.00	11.10	11.17	11.25	11.30	11.37	11.49	11.55	
PM.	12.05	12.12	12.23	12.30	12.45	12.55	x 1.00	z1.10	1.17	1.25	1.30	1.37	1.49	1.55	
	2.05	2.12	2.23	z2.30	2.45	2.55	x 3.00	3.10	3.17	3.25	3.30	3.37	3.49	3.55	
	4.05	4.12	4.23	4.30	4.45	4.55	x 5.00	5.10	5.17	5.25	5.30	5.37	5.49	5.55	
	6.05	6.12	6.23	6.30	6.45	6.55	x 7.00	7.10	7.17	7.25	7.30	7.37	7.49	7.55	
Freight A.M.	6.30	6.40	6.52	7.00	7.20	7.40	8.00	8.10	8.17	z8.35	8.42	8.50	9.00	9.07	9.15

†Not run Sundays.   xCross a Passenger Car.   zCross a Freight Car.   qSunday leaves at 8.05.

UNTIL FURTHER NOTICE EXTRA CARS WILL LEAVE
West Market Square 9.05a.m.   Morse's 9.11   Buckley's 9.23   Six Mile Falls 9.30
RETURNING WILL LEAVE
Six Mile Falls 9.30 a.m.   Buckley's 9.37   Morse's 9.49   West Market Square 9.55

College Boys Cured Of Taking Free Rides

THERE WAS A TIME that University of Maine college boys would catch free rides on the Old Town cars by hanging on the backs of the Libby fenders which were held in place by a stout steel hook. When they wanted to get off the car, they would haul the trolley down free of the wire.

To bring a halt to this practice, the company replaced the stout hooks with wire just strong enough to hold up the fender with little leeway for additional weight.

After several students latched onto the fenders and they fell to the ground, there were fewer riders on the rear of the cars!

NOTES ON THE ELECTRIC RAILWAYS OF MAINE

With 147 miles of track, the Lewiston, Augusta & Waterville Street Railway was Maine's most extensive street railway operation, followed by the Portland Railroad with 103 miles, Atlantic Store Line with 90 miles and the Bangor system placing fourth. The shortest electric road was the 2.1-mile Norway & Paris Street Raliway which never extended its original tracks.

The Pine Tree State had a total of slightly more than 520 miles of street railway lines, not all of which was in operation at any one time.

Several Maine street cars have been preserved at the Seashore Trolley Museum at Kennebunkport which has cars from the Mousam River, Atlantic Shore Line, Biddeford & Saco, Portland-Lewiston Interurban and the Aroostook Valley.

THE ELECTRIC RAILWAYS OF MAINE —Compiled by Charles D. Heseltine, 445 Preble Street, South Portland, Maine 04106.

	1st Yr.	
ATLANTIC SHORE LINE SYSTEM		
Mousam River Railroad	1893	Merged 1899 S&CP
Portsmouth, Kittery & York Street Railway	1897	Merged 1903 PD&Y
Sanford & Cape Porpoise Railway	1899	Atlantic Shore Line
Atlantic Shore Line Railway	1900	Atlantic Shore Ry. 1911
Kittery & Eliot Street Railway	1902	Merged 1903 PD&Y
Berwick & Eliot Street Railway	1903	N.H. portion of PD&Y
Berwick, Eliot & York Street Railway	1903	Renamed PD&Y
Portsmouth, Dover & York Street Railway	1903	Merged 1906 ASLRy
Atlantic Shore Railway	1911	York Utilities 1923
Portsmouth, Dover & York Street Railway	1917	Abandoned 1923
York Utilities Co.	1923	Pass. svc. aband. 1947
Aroostook Valley Railroad	1910	Conv. to diesel 1945-46
BANGOR SYSTEM		
Bangor Street Railway	1889	Became BR&E 1905
Bangor, Orono & Old Town Railway	1895	Became BR&E 1905
Bangor, Hampden & Winterport Railway	1896	Became BR&E 1905
Penobscot Central Railroad	1899	Bangor & Nor. 1905
Bangor & Northern Railroad	1905	Merged 1906 BR&E
Bangor Railway & Electric Co.	1905	Bangor Hydro 1925
Bangor Hydro Electric Co.	1925	Penobscot Trans 1940
Penobscot Transportation Co.	1940	Trolley until 1945
Biddeford & Saco Railroad	1888	Abandoned 1939
Calais Street Railway	1894	Abandoned 1929
Fryeburg Horse Railroad	1888	Aband. 1917
LEWISTON SYSTEM		
Lewiston & Auburn Horse Railroad	1881	Merged 1898 LB&B
Augusta, Hallowell & Gardiner Street Railway	1890	Merged 1902 AW&G
Augusta, Winthrop & Gardiner Street Railway	1902	Merged 1907 LA&W
Bath Street Railway	1893	Merged 1898 LB&B
Brunswick Electric Railroad	1896	Reorg. 1898 as LB&B
Lewiston, Brunswick & Bath Street Railway	1898	Became LA&W 1907
Portland & Brunswick Street Raliway	1902	Became B&Y 1911
Auburn & Turner Railroad	1905	Merged 1910 LA&W
Brunswick & Yarmouth Street Railway	1911	Merged 1913 LA&W
Lewiston, Augusta & Waterville St. Ry.	1907	Reorg. 1919 A&K
Turner Railroad	1920	Abandoned 1928
Androscoggin & Kennebec Railway	1919	Final operation 1941
PORTLAND RAILROAD COMPANY SYSTEM		
Portland & Forest Avenue Horse Railroad	1863	Became Port. RR 1865
Portland Railroad Company	1865	Leased 1912 CCP&L
Ocean Street Railroad (Deering)	1880	Merged 1885 Port. RR
Portland & Cape Elizabeth Railway	1895	Merged 1899 Port. RR
Portland & Yarmouth Electric Railway	1898	Merged 1900 Port. RR
Westbrook, Windham & Naples Railway	1899	Merged 1901 Port. RR
Cumberland County Power & Light Co.	1912	Last trolley 1941
Portland-Lewiston Interurban Railroad	1914	Abandoned 1933
Norway & Paris Street Railway	1895	Became Oxford Elec.
Oxford Electric Company	1916	Abandoned 1919
Rockland, Thomaston & Camden St. Ry.	1892	Knox Co. Elec. 1919
Knox County Electric Co.	1919	Abandoned 1931
Rockland, So. Thomaston & Owl's Head Ry.	1906	Reorganized 1908
Rockland, So. Thomaston & St. George Ry.	1908	Abandoned 1917
Skowhegan & Norridgewock Ry. & Power Co.	1894	Abandoned 1903
Somerset Traction Co.	1896	Skowhegan-Madison
WATERVILLE SYSTEM		
Waterville & Fairfield Horse Railroad	1888	Became W.&F.Ry.&Lt.
Waterville & Fairfield Railway & Light Co.	1891	Electrified 1892
Waterville & Oakland Street Railway	1903	Merged 1911
Waterville, Fairfield & Oakland Street Railway	1911	Abandoned 1937
Benton & Fairfield Railway	1898	Abandoned 1928
Fairfield & Shawmut Railway	1907	Abandoned 1927

Bangor's "Tin Bridge"

THE "TIN BRIDGE" in Bangor where Maine Central Railroad tracks crossed over the Hampden road is a landmark that gained notoriety by being a cause of the wreck of the "Bangor Express" on August 9, 1871.

The original bridge was a wooden Howe truss structure with track on its deck. Its wood covering was sheathed in tin for added protection from the elements—a fact that may have hastened the dry rot revealed in some of its shattered chords after the wreck. A brakeman and a passenger riding on one of the coach platforms were killed and 10 passengers were hurt.

The Maine Railroad Commissioners in their published investigative report took great care to absolve themselves of any responsibility for failing to check the condition of this span more thoroughly and insisted that the "fault of any deficiency was upon the road."

After sifting through numerous pages of testimony, the commission concluded that the train had been running downgrade at a speed faster than usual. Just before it got to the bridge the engineer had whistled for brakes, and the impact or "sudden jolt," the report said, of the brakes being applied just at the instant the train reached the bridge was sufficient cause for the easterly truss to give way in the center, sending five cars down to the Hampden road below.

In summation the Maine Railroad Commissioners expressed the fact that "it (the bridge) was not strong enough for the service exacted of it— but it should have been."

Rebuilt immediately after the wreck as a more substantial wooden structure, it was rebuilt of wrought iron in 1887, replaced as a steel structure in 1911, and in turn, rebuilt and widened in 1930. Yet the name "Tin Bridge" is still applied.